Parenting

Parenting: What really counts? examines the scientific evidence on what really matters for children's healthy psychological development.

The first part considers whether it is necessary to have two parents, a father present, parents who have a genetic link with their child, or parents who are heterosexual. Part two explores the psychological processes that underlie optimal development for children, particularly the quality of the child's relationship with parents, other family members and the wider social world. Contrary to common assumptions, Susan Golombok concludes that family structure makes less difference to children's psychological development than day-to-day experiences of family life.

As well as for students, researchers and teachers, *Parenting: What really counts?* will be of great interest to parents and those thinking of embarking on a non-traditional route to parenthood. It will also be welcomed by professionals working with families and those involved in the development of family policy.

Susan Golombok is Professor of Psychology and Director of the Family and Child Psychology Research Centre at City University, London. She is a leading international authority on the effects of non-traditional families on children's development. She is co-author of *Gender Development* (1994), *Growing up in a Lesbian Family* (1997) and *Modern Psychometrics* (second edition 1999).

Parenting

What really counts?

Susan Golombok

London and Philadelphia

First published 2000 by Routledge
11 New Fetter Lane, London EC4P 4EE

Simultaneously published in the USA and Canada
By Taylor & Francis Inc
325 Chestnut Street, Suite 800, Philadelphia, PA 19106

Routledge is an imprint of the Taylor & Francis Group

Typeset in Goudy by Keystroke, Jacaranda Lodge, Wolverhampton
Printed and bound in Great Britain by Biddles Ltd, Guildford and King's Lynn

British Library Cataloguing in Publication Data
A catalogue record for this book is available from the British Library

Library of Congress Cataloging in Publication Data
Golombok, Susan.
      Parenting : what really counts? / Susan Golombok.
         p.   cm.
      Includes bibliographical references and index.
      1. Parenting. 2. Parent and child. 3. Parents–Psychology. 4. Single
parents. 5. Gay parents. 6. Child psychology. I. Title.

HQ755.8 .G655 2000
649'.1–dc21   00-029096

ISBN 0–415–22715–1 (Hbk)
ISBN 0–415–22716–X (Pbk)

To my parents

Children of the future age,
Reading this indignant page,
Know that in a former time,
Love, sweet love, was thought a crime.
  (William Blake, 'A Little Girl Lost',
    from *Songs of Experience* (1793))*

*In *William Blake* (*The Oxford Authors*) edited by Michael Mason (1988) by permission of Oxford University Press.

Contents

Preface

This book was prompted by a growing number of telephone calls from the media asking for comment on questions such as 'How do children created as a result of surrogacy feel about their surrogate mother as they grow up?', 'Which mother do they see as their "real" mother?', 'Should children conceived by egg or sperm donation be told that their mother or father is not their genetic parent?', 'Will this information destroy their relationship with their non-genetic parent?', 'Should single women be allowed to become pregnant by donor insemination as their children will never know their father?', 'Do children need fathers?', 'Will children raised in lesbian families become lesbian or gay themselves?', 'Should gay men be allowed to adopt children?' and, following the birth of Dolly the sheep, 'Will cloning lead to a world without men?'

Three aspects of these questions were striking to me. First, it was assumed that the more families deviate from the norm of the traditional two-parent heterosexual family, the greater the risks would be to the child's psychological adjustment. Second, family structure was assumed to play a greater part in children's development than family process, that is, whether the family had one parent or two, whether or not a father was present, whether or not the child was genetically related to the parents, and whether the parents were heterosexual or homosexual, were considered to be more important than the quality of family relationships. Third, it was assumed that there was a simple relationship between non-traditional family structures and negative outcomes for children, for example, that one-parent families would produce delinquent children, lesbian families would produce sissy boys and tomboy girls, and families that lack a genetic relationship between the parents and the child would produce children who would always be hankering for their 'real' parents.

My aim in writing this book is to address the fundamental question 'What aspects of family life really matter for children's healthy psychological development?' In doing so, I hope to achieve two things. First, to present current research findings on the outcomes for children of being raised in different types of family structure. Although this involves the debunking of many myths (for example, the sons and daughters of lesbian and gay parents do not necessarily become lesbian and gay themselves, children of single mothers can grow up to be well-adjusted adults, and children raised by non-genetic parents are not confused about their identity), it also shows that the relationship between family structure and outcomes for children can be complex. For example, children born to single women on low income with little social support may be at high risk of developing behavioural problems, but children born to more affluent single women with a strong family network generally function well. The main message of the first half of the book is that family structure, in itself, does not play as important a part in children's development as is often thought. The aspects of children's development that are of interest differ from chapter to chapter. For children who lack a genetic link with their parents the main areas of concern are identity development and self-esteem, male and female sex-role behaviour and sexual orientation are of particular interest with lesbian families, and conduct disorder is often the focus of attention for children without fathers.

In Part I, quotes have been used to relay the thoughts and feelings of children and parents in different family types. These quotes have been extracted from the many interviews conducted at the Family and Child Psychology Research Centre at City University London over the past ten years. I am indebted to the interviewees for sharing their experiences with us, to the psychologists – Alison Bish, Rachel Cook, Emma Goodman, Fiona MacCallum, Clare Murray and Fiona Tasker – without whom some of the research discussed in this book would not have been undertaken, and to Margaret Pain. The names of interviewees have been changed to prevent identification.

In Part II, the processes within families that contribute towards positive or negative outcomes for children are examined. Chapter 5 focuses on attachment, highlighting what attachment is, why it is important, the consequences for children of secure versus insecure attachments to parents, and what we can learn from recent research about the intergenerational nature of attachment relationships, that is, the growing evidence that adults' views of their attachment relationships with their parents is predictive of the type of attachment relationships they have with their own children. The main conclusion here is that secure attachment relationships are of far-reaching importance for many aspects of psychological well-being in childhood and adult life but that attachment is not the whole story. Chapter 6 looks at the ways in which parents' relationship with each other, and their psychological state, can impact upon their relationship with their child. The focus of this chapter is on the mechanisms through which conflict between parents can result in emotional and behavioural problems in children, that is, as a direct effect of exposure to hostility between parents and as an indirect effect of the parents' hostility towards each other affecting their capacity to properly care for the child. Chapter 7 concentrates on the influence of children's experiences in the wider social world and addresses questions such as the effects of early day-care and of relationships with peers at school. The contribution of the child him or herself is also considered with particular attention to the child's temperament and capacity for resilience when circumstances are hard.

The main conclusion of the book, encapsulated in the final chapter, is that in considering what aspects of family life matter most for children's psychological well-being, more attention should be paid to the quality of family relationships and the child's relationships in the wider social world than simply to whether the child is being raised in one type of family or another. Another thread running through the book is the complexity of family life and the inappropriateness of assuming that just because children are raised in new family forms they are more likely to grow up psychologically disturbed, or that just because their family is a traditional one they will fare well. Emphasis is placed on the multiple influences on children's lives and the ways in which children's own characteristics interact with their experiences in the outside world.

I hope the book will be of interest to parents, and to those thinking of embarking on a non-traditional route to parenthood, as well as to professionals who work with families and who are involved in the development of family policy. It is not a self-help book but is intended to address the most common questions raised about different family types.

Part I

Family type

Chapter 1

Number of parents

One versus two?

Growing up in a single-parent family is generally considered to be bad for children, and yet more than 40 per cent of children find themselves in a single-parent family at some time during their school-age years. Does this mean that almost half of all children are at risk for psychological problems? Or are single parent families not so harmful after all?

Single mothers are often portrayed as young unmarried women who are financially dependent on the state. Indeed, this is the image of single parents that commonly comes to mind. But it is just as inaccurate to describe all single mothers in this way as it is to depict all married parents as financially and emotionally secure. Single-parent families are as diverse as are two-parent families. Even Diana, Princess of Wales, was a single mother. Children being raised by single parents are to be found everywhere.

> 'At his school there are parents who are actors, television producers and famous people, and in my daughter's class nearly all of them are single parents. When I get speaking to some of these mothers – and you should see their houses, really beautiful – a lot of fathers are just not there. This fallacy about single parents being income supported, unemployable people or stupid teenagers, it's just not true. It's rare for my daughter to go to a house and the father is there.'

Single-parent families are formed in a variety of ways. Although most result from the parents' separation or divorce, some lose a parent through death, and others have had only one parent right from the start. As the large majority of single-parent families are headed by a mother rather than a father, single-mother families will be the focus of this chapter. Fathers bringing up children alone will be discussed in Chapter 2.

How single mothers feel about their lives depends to a large extent on their experiences, but many are positive about single parenthood even in the face of extreme hardship.

'Today its easy, tomorrow it might be difficult. If a friend of mine said "Should I be a single mother?", I would say "No". But I wouldn't change my circumstances, not for anything in the world. That's not to say there haven't been times, you know, when it all gets too much. It's a huge task and I had no idea. I don't think anyone does until you have a baby. You've no conception of it.'

'You have to be all things to all people. You can never be ill, you can never be tired and you can never run out of resources even when you are on your knees. If I was confronted with the same choices I would do it again, but I wouldn't choose it as a way of life.'

Children's experiences in single-parent families vary enormously. Many such children are accepting of their upbringing.

'It's not something I bother about. So many people I know have single parents. I think among people I know it's more unusual if their parents are together so it's not really been a problem for me you know.'

'A lot of my friends were in the same boat. In my class at school out of about thirty kids there were only three or four who had a mum and dad there.'

'I have a strong relationship with my mother, very strong. People are amazed how close I am to my mother and how we can just talk about things openly. They think it's really sweet that I've got that special relationship with my mother when they haven't with either of their parents.'

But for other children, life in a single-parent family can be hard.

'I blamed it on her. The fact that my dad wasn't there. That probably wasn't right but she was the only one there to take the blame, you know, to take it out on I suppose.'

'I felt embarrassed about the fact that my mum and dad weren't married and I didn't know who my dad was. For a long time I was very embarrassed about it.'

'The only situation I didn't like was at school when children said they went out with their dad on their birthday or at Christmas. I didn't worry about the things I got, it was just the thought of not having a dad to be with, to go out with and everything else. That was the worst time at school but I wasn't ashamed to say that I was from a one-parent family.'

'I missed it when other people at school said "My dad this" and "My dad that". That's when it used to hit me and I would think "If only I had a dad" you know.

I wished my dad was there when I got home from school or to help me with my homework. I did miss out on that.'

Many single parents suffer extreme financial difficulties, but not all do. Some receive a great deal of help from family and friends while others do not. And some mothers choose to go it alone whereas others find themselves thrust involuntarily into single parenthood. As we shall see from the research discussed below, the outcomes for children in single-parent families depend to a large extent on the circumstances of their lives.

Divorced and separated single-mother families

Most single-parent families result from marital breakdown, and children whose parents divorce are more likely to have psychological problems and are less likely to perform well at school than children in non-divorced families.[1] Mavis Hetherington and her colleagues in the United States followed up a group of 4-year-old children from the time of their parents' divorce. These children were compared with two groups of children whose parents remained together; in one group the parents had a happy marriage, and in the other the parents did not get on. The behaviour of all of the children was assessed both at home and at school over a period of six years.[2,3]

In the first year, the children from divorced families were functioning less well than their counterparts from intact families – even than those whose parents did not get on. The children from divorced families were more aggressive, defiant, distractible, demanding and lacking in self-control, both at home and at school, than the children from two-parent families.

However, by the end of the second year, the situation had changed. It was the boys from intact but unhappy two-parent families who showed the highest level of aggression and defiance, although the sons of divorced parents were still functioning less well than boys from harmonious two-parent homes. The girls from divorced families had returned to normal by this time. There was very little difference between them and the girls from two-parent homes where the parents got on well. A similar situation was found six years after the divorce. Compared with children in non-divorced families, daughters whose mothers had not remarried remained well adjusted. Sons, although improved, still tended to be more non-compliant, impulsive and aggressive in their behaviour.

There is no doubt that divorce is difficult and upsetting for children, and many experience emotional and behavioural problems around this time. But it seems that within two years most children of divorced parents have adapted fairly well. Couples are often encouraged to stay together for the sake of the children. But is it really true that a 'bad' marriage is better for children than divorce? Or do children fare better if their parents separate? Although every family is different, it appears that in the long run it is not always a good idea for parents to remain in a hostile marriage just for the children's sake. If divorce leads to an improved relationship between the parents, divorce can be beneficial for all concerned. But if parents remain in conflict after the divorce, the evidence suggests that it is better for children if their parents do not part.[4]

What aspects of divorce are most likely to lead to problems for children? Is it the divorce itself? Is it living in a single-parent family after the divorce? Or is it something else entirely that is at the root of children's difficulties? It used to be assumed that the higher incidence of psychological problems and poorer academic performance of children from divorced families was due to separation from a parent. But the finding that children who had lost a parent through death did not show such difficulties led psychologists to conclude that it is not so much separation as exposure to conflict and hostility between parents that is the key factor in contributing to children's distress.[5]

Further evidence for this explanation came from comparisons between children from happy and unhappy two-parent families. Children in two-parent families whose parents were in conflict were much more likely to show behavioural and emotional problems than those whose parents had a harmonious relationship.[5] Interestingly, studies that have followed children through childhood have shown that they can begin to show problems years before the divorce actually takes place, sometimes even before the parents have considered separation.[6] This tells us that the psychological problems shown by children when their parents divorce do not simply result from the divorce itself but instead arise in response to the arguments and bitterness between parents that they experience at home. It is also entirely possible, and in some cases very likely, that the behavioural and emotional problems shown by children whose parents are in conflict actually contribute to the breakdown of the marriage. For those couples whose relationship is in difficulty, the presence of non-compliant and aggressive children is unlikely to create a situation that is conducive to resolving their marital problems.

The financial hardship that commonly accompanies the transition into a single-parent family after divorce is another important factor associated with children's psychological problems and poorer performance at school. As part of a study of all 16,000 children born in England and Wales in a week in March 1958, Elsa Ferri compared children in single-parent families with children in two-parent families around the time of their eleventh birthday.[7] She found that the children in single-parent families were more likely to have emotional and behavioural problems and to be doing less well at school. But the difficulties faced by children living with single mothers could be explained almost entirely by the low income associated with single parenthood rather than the absence of a parent. When family income was taken into account, children in single-parent families were no different from children with two parents in the family home.

More recently Sara McLanahan and Gary Sandefur conducted a detailed examination of four large, nationally representative samples in the USA and concluded that the lower income (and the sudden drop in income) that results from lone parenthood is the single most important factor in the underachievement of young people from single-parent homes.[8] They found that adolescents who had lived apart from one parent during some period of their childhood were twice as likely to drop out of high school, twice as likely to have a child before the age of 20, and one and a half times more likely to be out of work in their late teens or early twenties than those from a similar background who grew up with two parents at home.

For the majority of single parents it is a constant struggle to make ends meet, and many feel that it is lack of money which is largely responsible for the problems they experience in bringing up their children.

'The disadvantage of being a single parent is that the level of child support is ridiculously low which forces people like myself to go out and do little bitty jobs which takes away the time from your child – just to survive.'

'The first two years were sheer hell. Wonderful in some ways but sheer hell in terms of lack of sleep and lack of finances. I think there's more stress associated with lack of money than anything else. It undermines you completely. You feel worthless, you feel you're not coping. You feel you're not caring for you child. It's a horrible feeling.'

It is not just financial support but social support that is often lacking for single mothers. The absence of a father from the home often leaves the mother with no one else to share the day-to-day tasks of raising a child.

'When she was a baby buying a loaf of bread was a big issue because if she was asleep did you wake her or decide to go without the bread? If there is someone else there you can go out. So to that extent there is strain.'

'Occasionally it would be nice to say "I'm going out for an hour, they're yours". I can never do that ever which is difficult sometimes.'

'The thing about being a single parent is that you can doubt yourself. You wonder whether you are doing it right. You don't get feedback. If your child behaves badly you think it must be something you've done wrong. I think as a single parent you are not always consistent. You don't always want to be the one doing the telling off.'

Another reason for children's problems in the months following divorce is that this is when mothers often feel at their most vulnerable.[9] It is not unusual for mothers to feel anxious, depressed, lonely and lacking in confidence when they divorce. At the same time children become more demanding, less compliant, more aggressive and more withdrawn. For newly single mothers the demands of looking after difficult children while in a poor emotional state themselves can be more than they can take, and their ability to function as effective parents may diminish at this time. They may be less affectionate, less communicative, more irritable and more punitive to their children than ever before which, in turn, may exacerbate their children's difficulties in adjusting to divorce.

But the improvement in children's adjustment following divorce is paralleled by an improvement in the emotional well-being of their mothers. Mavis Hetherington found that by two years following divorce three-quarters of divorced women reported that they were happier in their new situation than they had been in the final year of their marriage, and most felt that it was easier to raise their children alone than with a disengaged, undermining or acrimonious husband.[9]

> 'There have been hairy moments. I feel I've been to hell and back. And something very strong inside you emerges when you actually think you've been through the worst. It can only get better from now on.'

> 'Our circumstances have changed very dramatically by my own design. We were in dire, dire straits, and now we live a very comfortable existence. We have lived through some tough times together, him and I, and we have come out at the other end.'

Not all children experience problems in adjusting to divorce. Nor do all children who do develop problems improve within two years. Whether or not children will develop difficulties, and how quickly they will recover, depends on a number of factors.[10] We have seen that boys generally appear to be more vulnerable than girls although it has been suggested that girls may show their distress in different ways. Children's age at the time of divorce also seems to make a difference, with adolescence being a particularly difficult time. But of particular importance is the effect of the divorce on the relationship between parents. When parents remain in conflict after the divorce children are more likely to continue to have problems, especially if they are drawn into disagreements. But divorce can improve the situation between parents, and when this happens the outlook for children is much better. The quality of the relationship between the child and the parents also makes a difference. A warm and supportive relationship with at least one parent after the divorce goes a long way towards protecting the child.

In the past, the custody of children following divorce was generally awarded to only one parent, usually the mother, and the custodial parent had absolute power to decide whether or not the child should have contact with the other parent. The reasoning behind this view was that children need to have a secure relationship with at least one parent, and that children whose parents divorce would have difficulty in relating to two parents who are hostile towards each other. It was thought that conflicts of loyalty would arise for children that would destroy their relationship with both parents. In recent years, opinion on this issue has changed following the findings of Mavis Hetherington and others pointing to better outcomes for children who have a positive relationship with their non-custodial parent.[10] The courts now consider that it is desirable for children to have a continuing relationship with both parents, and there has been a move towards giving greater access to the non-custodial parent and, to a lesser extent, towards awarding custody jointly to both parents.

Little research has been conducted on the effects of different types of custody arrangements for children, and the studies that have been carried out have failed to produce clear and consistent results. It seems that whether or not the parents remain in conflict after the divorce has a greater influence on the outcome for the child than the type of custody arrangement. Irrespective of custody arrangements, children whose mother and father can co-operate over parenting adjust more easily to divorce.[9,10]

Solo mothers

In recent years the greatest increase in single parents has been among unmarried mothers. Some unmarried mothers live with the father of their child and are not single parents at all, but a growing number have been single right from the start. Although many of these women did not plan to have children, or had assumed that the father would be involved in parenting, it is becoming more and more common for women to actively choose to have children on their own. Most planned children of single mothers are conceived in the usual way, but some women attend an infertility clinic and conceive their child using the sperm of an anonymous donor.[11] One reason given by single women for opting for this procedure is to avoid using a man to produce a child without his knowledge or consent. Donor insemination also means that they do not have to share the rights and responsibilities for the child with a man to whom they are not emotionally attached.

The experiences of children raised by mothers who have been single from the start differ in some ways from those of children who find themselves in a single-parent family because of divorce. First, they have not been separated from a parent with whom they had shared their daily lives and, more importantly, they have not been exposed to conflict and hostility between their mother and father. Second, they have not experienced the emotional distress and reduced involvement in parenting that is common among single mothers at the time of divorce. For these reasons we might expect children raised from birth by single mothers to be less at risk for psychological problems and underachievement at school than children who find themselves in single-mother families because of divorce. But other factors associated with difficulties for children in single-parent families such as low income and lack of social support are just as likely to occur in families where the mother has been single from the outset. In addition, children in these more unusual single-mother families may be more likely to be teased or bullied at school than children whose single-mother family has resulted from divorce.

Research on solo-mother families is of interest because the findings tell us what happens to children raised by only one parent right from birth. As yet only a few such studies have been carried out, some with only small numbers of volunteers, but the findings are beginning to shed some light on the outcomes for children in these circumstances. As part of her large study of one-parent families in the UK, Elsa Ferri examined children raised from birth by a single mother and tentatively concluded that these children were as well adjusted as children in two-parent families.[7] A recent study, also in the UK, by myself and my colleagues Fiona Tasker and Clare Murray, focused on the quality of family relationships and the emotional well-being of children raised from infancy by financially secure single mothers.[12] It was found that the children experienced greater warmth and involvement with their mother, and were more securely attached to her, than a comparison group of children from two-parent homes. However, the children felt less competent in both physical and intellectual activities.

In the United States, McLanahan and Sandefur reported rather more negative findings when they looked at young people who had been raised by unmarried mothers,[8] but the researchers emphasised that this was largely due to the economic disadvantage they had experienced while growing up. In a small but in-depth study of financially secure single mothers who had raised their children alone since birth, also in the United States, Marsha Weinraub and her colleagues showed that more negative outcomes for children appear to be associated with the low levels of social support and high levels of stress experienced by these mothers; the mothers who were most under stress and most lacking in social support were those whose children were most at risk.[13]

Women who raise their children alone from the outset encounter difficulties over and above those of mothers who become single later in life.

> 'I've found parenting a very natural process but I think it's phenomenally taxing to do it well. It's very, very demanding. And it's been exceptionally demanding for me because I had my child before I finished my education, and I had to pursue my education in order to get the kind of work I wanted. So I had to study. I had to pay for that myself. I had to work full-time. I worked the most horrendous hours – forty, fifty, sixty hours per week and weekends with no holidays. I found it incredibly demanding, that combination of more than a full-time job and being a full-time parent.'

But just like those for whom divorce has led to single motherhood, solo mothers who feel supported by their family and friends find single parenting a much easier undertaking than those who have no one to turn to.

> 'My mum kept me alive financially for the first four years of my son's life and then I took over my own finances and sorted my life out. Moral support was absolute. I get a lot of backing from my family.'

> 'I get enormous support from friends. Most of my friends are single parents and I also have a couple of fellows who are my friends. They are really good with my son. And if I really have a big problem one of them will take it on and have a chat with him, man to man. I have masses of support and I think that is probably the most important thing.'

Many solo mothers feel there are certain advantages to raising their children alone.

'I feel I am doing as well as anybody. Financially it is more difficult. But on the other hand there are positive things about bringing up a child on your own because I don't have the demands of anyone else. Although I don't have anyone to share the responsibility, I don't have anybody who I don't agree with over things. Lots of people I know who are in couples have tensions between them as a couple and also over childrearing. That is very evident.'

'I don't think I've had any more difficulties than a lot of my friends who have a partner. A lot of their difficulties have been about the impact of a child on their relationship. And in a couple of cases that has destroyed the relationship between the two adults.'

One challenge facing solo mothers that does not exist for single mothers following divorce is that they have to answer their children's questions about who their father is and why he does not live with them.

'I made it quite clear about why he isn't with us. And I also wanted it to be very clear that it wasn't that he wouldn't marry me. I didn't want it to come over that I was dumped and that I got lumbered with a baby. Although that is what happened in a way I feel that I got the good end of the deal. I got a beautiful child.'

'I told her from quite an early age that her daddy had run away, at about 2½ years old when she became aware of other children having daddies. And I would get quite weepy myself when I saw friends' children's fathers coming home and getting all excited and she didn't have that.'

Although children generally accept that there is no father in their life many are curious about who their father is.

'When I was at secondary school it wasn't a really bad thing. There were a few that didn't have fathers. It didn't really bother me. It was only when I started getting older that I went through a phase where I just wanted to find out who he was. I was going to go here, there and everywhere, to Citizens Advice, to try and trace him. I think it was because I wasn't getting on with my mum and I thought that if I found my dad then he'd understand. So I think I was just going through a phase where I just wanted to hurt my mum. I wanted to get my dad and then I would be happy.'

'My mum said I could see him when I was 16. Now when I was 16 she said we'll leave it until you're 18 and you can do what you want, it was left at that.

So I had another two years to wait. It was like a climax because you get images you know and I had images of this rich man. He is rich you know but he looked a bit old. This year he just rung up my mum out of the blue and said "Let's have dinner". I was nervous when we went out to dinner but it was nice, it was all right you know. I was pleased to see him after all these years, but at the same time I felt very jealous because I felt that the only reason he contacted us was to see my mum and not me.'

'Recently I've started to think "Well I wonder if I will trace him one day". One day I might find the urge, you know, to go and find him. I know that I could probably find him fairly easily if I wanted to because my mother is still friends with some of his family. It's all a bit hazy because I'm not really sure if he knows of my existence or he doesn't. I mean it's not something that I want to push with my mum. I don't know why but I don't really want to discuss it with her. She has told me but I sort of block it out. I don't really feel anything towards him. Sometimes I feel quite cold towards him. Then I think if I traced him, if he's got other family, a wife and children, if he didn't know anything about it, it could cause a lot of ructions in someone's life and his family might not be very happy about it, so I'd have to go very carefully. I wouldn't go barging over there and say "I am your daughter that you didn't know about".'

But not all children want to find their father.

'If you're born into a situation where you don't know anything other than your mother it doesn't seem any different to you. I suppose when I started school I suddenly realised "I don't have a dad", and I think I twigged from about 5 or 6 that other people had a dad and I didn't but it didn't play a tremendously big part in my life. I just accepted it because I had my mum.'

'I never knew my father. He deserted my mum before I was born so I've never seen him to this day. I've never had a father. My mum's been really good. You know she's been mum and dad to me. There was a stage I was going through when I wanted to find my father because I've been told that I am like him in a lot of ways. I think it was just curiosity really. I obviously wanted to know the story and my mum told me, and when she told me I went off him you know. I don't think he wanted me, he wanted me aborted, so if it hadn't have been for her I wouldn't be here talking to you now.'

All these children know that they have a father somewhere. Even if they never meet him the possibility always exists. They can also ask their mother about their father and build up a picture of him in their mind. But for children conceived using the sperm of an anonymous donor there is no possibility of ever making contact with their father. How these children will feel about their origins as they grow up remains, as yet, to be seen.

Are single-parent families bad for children?

It seems that children in one-parent families are less likely to do well at school and are more likely to develop psychological problems than children in two-parent families. This does not mean that all children raised by single mothers will have difficulties, but it does mean that they are more at risk. Thus the widely held belief that children in single-parent families are at a disadvantage compared with children from two-parent homes is borne out by the findings of research.

But is it having only one parent, in itself, that is bad for children? Or are other aspects of single parenthood responsible for their problems? For children who find themselves in a single-parent family because of divorce, it seems that the conflict between parents before and after the divorce, as well as the mother's reduced ability to function effectively as a parent when she herself is feeling vulnerable, are often at the root of children's difficulties. And whether or not the single-parent family has resulted from divorce, many lone mothers experience severe financial hardship and have little social support, both of which have been implicated in children's problems.

A further explanation that cannot be ruled out (although difficult to test) is that the differences between children in one-parent and two-parent households may result from differences between the characteristics of parents in these two family types. It has also been suggeted that differences between the children may reflect genetic rather than environmental influences, and that these genetic influences may be associated with both single-parenthood and poorer outcomes for children. Genetic influences on family relationships and child development will be discussed in Chapter 7.

It appears that it is not so much the absence of a parent but the difficulties that come with it that lead to adverse outcomes for the child. The findings of research on children whose mothers have been single from the start, and who are financially secure with supportive family and friends, will tell us more about whether growing up in a one-parent family, in itself, is bad for children. In the meantime, what is clear is that the circumstances of single-mother families can be just as diverse as those of two-parent families, and it seems that it is the circumstances in which these families find themselves, rather than the absence of a parent, that matter most for the child.

Chapter 2

Fathers

Present or not?

If children in single-parent families are at a disadvantage compared with those in two-parent homes this suggests that fathers play an important part in their children's lives. But is the father's contribution only to provide an income and to give emotional support to the mother? Or do fathers also have a direct influence on their children's development? And is it fathers' maleness that is important? Or is it their involvement as an additional parent in the home?

Before looking at fathers' relationships with their children it must be acknowledged that their role as providers of economic and social support is a very important one. The less women have to worry about how to pay the bills, and the more they feel they can talk over the ups and down of family life with someone close, the better they feel, and the better they function as mothers. But in this chapter we are considering what fathers do directly with their children, and what difference contact between fathers and their children really makes.

What fathers do

In recent years we have heard a great deal about the 'new father', a father who spends time with his children, shows a real interest in them, and shares in the day-to-day chores of bringing them up. But does he actually exist? Or is he simply a product of media hype and mothers' wishful thinking? Although there has been some increase in fathers' involvement with their children, the changes that have taken place are not as great as we are sometimes led to believe. It is still the case that raising children remains largely in the mother's domain. Michael Lamb, an eminent researcher on fathering, reported in 1997 that in two-parent families where the mother does not go out to work, fathers spend less than a quarter of the time that mothers do with their children.[1] In families where the mother is employed, fathers spend a slightly higher proportion of time, about one-third that of mothers. But this is not because fathers are doing more; employed mothers are doing less.

> 'If I've got fault as a father that's what it is. I don't make the time. When I finish work I tend to pop over to the local and have a couple of quick ones. I tend to go over there after work, unwind, have a couple of jars, come back, and my

dinner's ready. Then I have to do more work. My daughter sees her friends after school and then does her homework in front of the television or in her room. I'll come in for the 9 o'clock news. Other than that, unless there's a bit of football on, I'm not a great lover of television. It is difficult running your own business from home.'

'When I was working I was never here. I used to go at 6.30 in the morning and come home at midnight sometimes. So I only got to see them at the weekend.'

'I've been working very hard these last few years. It's very hard sometimes to come home and have to start up doing things when all I really want to do is sit down. So I find it a bit hard.'

Michael Lamb distinguishes between three aspects of involvement with children – actual contact, being available, and taking responsibility for organising childcare when the parents are not at home.[2,3] It has been estimated that fathers' actual contact time is approximately two hours per day on weekdays and six-and-a-half hours on Sundays, and that their availability is around four hours per day on weekdays and ten hours on Sundays. By the time children reach adolescence, direct contact has reduced to less than one hour on weekdays and two hours on Sundays. Fathers also take little responsibility for arranging childcare. It is almost always mothers, not fathers, who stay at home when their children are unwell, who take their children to the doctor, who make sure they take a bath and brush their teeth, and who find a babysitter when they want to go out. In families where both parents are employed fathers are slightly more involved with their children but, in comparison with mothers, they still lag far behind.

'He'll take the option of not doing anything if I am there to do it. I can't ever imagine him getting our son his dinner. Last night I had to go to a playgroup meeting and I put my son to bed and washed up before I went out.'

'I know that he's there if necessary but he's not around very much. Physically I feel that it's all left to me. I seem to do all the running around and fetching or carrying.'

It seems that even when fathers are in the company of their children, they interact with them less than do mothers. Jay Belsky and Brenda Volling observed parents at home and found that mothers responded to, stimulated, showed affection to and cared for their baby more than did fathers. The only activities that fathers engaged in more than mothers were reading and watching television.[4]

'If he's in and she's playing with something I'll say "Let daddy see" or "Go and read that book to daddy" or "Here's your library book. Daddy will maybe read it to you". This will happen a couple of times a week. I think he enjoys it. He doesn't jump up and down and clap his hands or anything. But he's very proud of her.'

'They've got a good relationship. My husband's not a terribly demonstrative person and for a while she didn't like going out with him. She'd rather be with me. But when she's with him they get on well and they cuddle up together. She's with him every Friday night when I go out. It's very good. It does them both good. On the census form I filled in that at a conservative estimate he did 105 hours' work the week before the census. So there's not a lot of time left over. If she is to see him it's usually on a Friday night. Quite often when I come back the two of them are sound asleep.'

The finding that mothers are more likely to interact with their children than fathers holds true even in less traditional families. In Sweden, fathers have the option of taking time off work to look after their new-born baby instead of mothers, and Michael Lamb and his colleagues were able to compare families where the father had taken leave for more than one month with families who had opted for the more usual situation where the mother stayed at home.[5] The researchers visited these families when the baby was 3 months, 8 months and 16 months old, and observed what the mother and the father each did with the baby. Even in families where it was the father who took leave, mothers were more likely to hold, touch, tickle, talk to and be affectionate with the baby when they were at home. And interestingly, of the twenty-six fathers who intended to take leave for at least one month, only seventeen actually did so when the time came. A similar situation was found in Israeli kibbutz families where both parents worked and children were brought up communally. Mothers were found be more affectionate and talkative to their babies than fathers, and looked after them more during their time at home.[6]

It is not just with babies that fathers are less involved. In a study of parents of 6- to 7-year-old children, mothers were shown to be available to their children for fifty-five hours per week compared with fathers' thirty-five hours.[7] And when it came to spending time alone with their children, the twenty-two hours per week of mothers' time hugely exceeded the two hours put in by fathers. By adolescence, little has changed: 15- and 16-year-olds spend more than twice as much time alone with their mother than they do with their father.[8]

Fathers differ from mothers not only in how much time they spend with their children but also in what they do when they are with them.[9,10] Whereas mothers spend much of their time caring for children – feeding them, bathing them and helping with homework – fathers spend a greater proportion of their time in play. The way in which they play is also different. Fathers are much more physical and boisterous when playing with their young children, especially with their sons, than are mothers. Mothers more often play quietly with toys. And as children grow up, fathers are more likely to take part in active, outdoor play with their children than are mothers.

'I take him to football, we go water-skiing, and snow skiing. I go and watch him play football as well. We play table tennis, sometimes we have a game of pool, and we play chess.'

'If I'm out in the shed he'll come out and say "OK dad can I make this?", and we'll knock something up.'

'So far he's left most of it up to me. I get her dinner and see to her daily needs. The only things he'll take part in are discipline and play.'

It seems that fathers are young children's preferred playmates, not just for boys but for girls as well. In a study of 2½-year-olds, Alison Clarke-Stewart found that when given the choice of who to play with, more than two-thirds of the children chose their father in preference to their mother.[11] Michael Lamb's research on younger children produced the same finding. His observational studies of families at home show that right from infancy, babies prefer to play with their dad.[9]

Nevertheless, in absolute terms, mothers still spend more hours per week playing with children than do fathers.[1] In addition, fathers' greater involvement in play, and their preference for boisterous play, may be specific to certain cultures.[10] In Sweden and Israel, where parents have less traditional family roles, no differences have been identified between mothers and fathers in the amount or type of play they engage in with their children.

Fathers' relationships with their adolescent children also differ from those of mothers. As well as spending less time with their father than with their mother, teenagers see their father as more distant and more controlling, have fewer conversations with him, and tell him less than they tell their mother about what is happening in their lives.[8]

'If something was bothering her she would probably talk to her mother first rather than me.'

'We don't talk a great deal. I've always been available but we have never really conversed at any great length or depth. I used to read to them a lot when they were younger.'

'If something was worrying her I don't think she would tell me. I think she would allow her mum to drag it out of her. I don't think that she would come to me with it.'

Nevertheless, fathers who are there when things go wrong can provide a sense of security for the family. They can also be a source of authority in children's lives.

'If I get into trouble my mum just gets upset and shouts at me. But dad listens to what I have to say. He doesn't shout at me, although he cares that

I have done wrong, and helps me sort the problem out. At these times I love my dad more.'

Are fathers incompetent?

Because fathers are less involved with their children, particularly when it comes to day-to-day care, does this mean that they are less competent parents? It seems not. As we shall see in Chapter 5, in the first year of life it is important that parents are sensitive to their infants' needs and respond appropriately to their cries and smiles. In this way infants come to view their parents as a source of comfort and become securely attached to them. To test whether fathers are as responsive as mothers, Ross Parke and Douglas Sawin observed parents interacting with their infants while feeding them.[12] They found that fathers were just as sensitive as mothers to their infants' coos of pleasure and cries of distress, and were just as likely to respond appropriately by touching, looking at or talking to them, or by removing the cause of their discomfort. Also, infants drank just as much milk when fed by their father as by their mother, so clearly fathers were doing something right.

Fathers are also able to care for their school-age children as well as mothers. Graeme and Alan Russell interviewed parents of 6- and 7-year-old children about how often they helped with the child's homework, made a packed lunch, put the child to bed, played, and sat down with the child to have a talk or a cuddle.[7] Mothers and fathers were also observed with their child at home and ratings were made of how often each parent took part in a shared activity with the child, explained how something worked, expressed warmth towards the child, or showed disapproval of the child's behaviour. Although mothers spent more time with their children, particularly in caring for them, fathers were just as warm and responsive to their children and were no more likely than mothers to discipline them for misbehaviour. On most days fathers had a cuddle, went over the child's day and sat down to have a chat.

'We talk about her day and what she has done at school. Usually there will be some latest project, which she'll want to get on with and will bully me into doing this, that or the other that needs to be done for the project. Or it may be having to go out and buy things in order to do the project. So there is quite a lot of that kind of activity, Can I find this? Or do that?'

'We chat every day. He'll come in and sit down and I'll ask how school has gone, and he'll say we did this today and that today. We will talk about football or anything to do with sport.'

'I know when there is something wrong with him, just by looking at him. Just by his manner I know there's something wrong.'

So it seems that fathers are as capable as caring for their children as mothers – they just do it less. Further evidence for their competence comes from research on infants' attachment to their parents.[9] Infants who are in unfamiliar situations, or in the presence of an unfamiliar person, tend to seek out and stay close to their attachment figures – the people they trust. By observing infants' reactions to the presence of a stranger, Michael Lamb has shown that infants turn to their father as well as to their mother. Although babies are more likely to want their mother than their father when they are feeling wary or upset, when the mother is not there the father can be a source of comfort and allay distress.

> 'My son is affectionate with my husband but not in the same way as he is with me. It's more sort of play cuddles when they're fighting. They are affectionate together but it's different. If my son hurts himself he wants me.'

Babies' tendency to turn to their mother rather than their father in times of stress is most likely due to their greater contact with her. The more fathers become involved with their infants, the more their infants are likely to seek comfort from them instead. This was demonstrated by Martha Cox and her colleagues who investigated fathers' relationships with their babies, first when they were aged 3 months and again at 1 year old.[13] The fathers who took delight in their 3-month-old infants, and who were affectionate and encouraging to them, were most likely to have securely attached 1-year-olds. It seems that there is nothing special about what mothers do with their babies. If fathers do the same they too can have a close bond with their child.

> 'She is very affectionate. She shows it by cuddles and making fun of me. And then I respond in the same way. She teases me and I tease her. I feel very cuddly towards her and she does towards me. It's very much equal. I often say to her "I hope you'll always stay this way, you know, cuddly".'

> 'Very often when I go up to say goodnight to her the lights are off and this little face peeps out at me and literally my heart does miss a beat.'

> 'I have said to the children "There's no point in having children if you can't cuddle them" and I say "Right, if I can't have a cuddle you might as well leave. Go now! No point in you living here unless I can come up and give you big wet kisses and cuddles". I do feel that at times. I love them and, you know, as far as I'm concerned I want them to give me a cuddle when I want to give them a cuddle. When she goes to bed at night it is she who will come down and kiss me. And we have silly games. Sometimes I say "No, I'm not kissing children today, all kisses are off" so that she will force herself to give me a kiss. I get better kisses that way!'

But not all fathers find it easy to be affectionate. Showing their feelings, and talking to their children about feelings, does not always come naturally.

'I can't cuddle him. I'm not that type of person. I had a very bad childhood so I'm not a cuddling person. I show my affection by buying him something, or taking him out, or treating him, rather than by cuddling. I find it very hard. I always give him a cuddle in the morning and a cuddle when I come home at night but I find it difficult to show affection in that way. That's the way I was brought up. I get more enjoyment by taking him out and buying him something and showing my love that way. That's just me. That's the way I am.'

'I'm not a particularly demonstrative person in terms of affection so it's more a case of her coming up and giving me hugs than me giving her hugs.'

'I don't think I'm a brilliant dad. When my son and I have a row and he goes off to his room in tears I should really go after him. Really we should sit down and discuss what the problem is and go over it. The trouble is I cop out.'

What difference do fathers make?

We have seen that fathers can be just as effective parents as mothers, but how much difference do fathers really make to the development of their children? This question has been examined in three ways. First, fatherless families have been studied to see whether children without fathers differ from those who grow up with their father at home. Second, research has been carried out on families headed by a single father, and on families with highly involved fathers, to see what effect this has on the child. The idea is that if children in these families do better or worse than other children in certain ways, this will tell us how fathers influence their children. Third, ordinary two-parent families have been studied to help us understand how different aspects of fathers' relationships with their children affect children's well-being.

As we saw in Chapter 1, children raised by single mothers are more likely than children in two-parent households to have psychological problems and perform poorly at school, difficulties that are often blamed on the absence of a father from the family. But how much can be attributed to the absence of a father in itself? And is it specifically his maleness that matters? Or is it the absence of a second parent from the home? In Chapter 1 we saw that many factors are associated with the problems experienced by children raised by single mothers – conflict between parents, the loss of a parent from the family, economic hardship, the mother's emotional distress and her lack of social support. All of these factors are linked with the absence of a father but we cannot say whether it is the lack of a parent in general, or the lack of a male parent in particular, that is responsible for the difficulties faced by children in single-mother homes.

Can studying single-mother families tell us anything at all about the specific role of fathers in children's development? Fathers are often thought to have a unique influence on children's sex-role behaviour. If so, we might expect that girls in fatherless families would be less feminine, and boys less masculine, than children who grow up with both their mother and their father in the family home. In fact, father absence appears to make little difference to sex-role development for either boys or girls. Most children raised by single mothers are typical of their sex and, in their choice of toys, games and activities, are just like boys and girls from two-parent homes.[14] As we shall see in Chapter 4, it seems that parents make little difference to the masculinity or femininity of their daughters and sons, so a father's maleness, in itself, does not seem to play a unique part in the development of his child.

What can we learn from families where the father takes on what has traditionally been the mother's role? Although far less common than single-mother families, some children are brought up by single fathers. This is most likely to occur when the mother has died, or after the parents' separation or divorce. It is very unusual for fathers to be awarded custody of their children after divorce, and when this does happen the mother is usually unable to care for them herself, often due to physical or mental illness. Because so few single-father families exist, there has been little research on what happens to the children. But the few studies that have been carried out show that most single fathers are able to care for their children well.[15] In fact, there is some evidence that after divorce boys adjust better when they live with their father than with their mother. But it is important to remember that fathers who have custody of their children, particularly those who choose custody rather than have custody thrust upon them, are likely to have had good relationships with them before the divorce. Single fathers are also more likely to receive offers of help and be praised for their efforts than single mothers who are often subjected to criticism and hostility from the outside world. Although these families are unusual, it does seem that single fathers can make good parents, particularly for their sons.

Studies of highly involved fathers in two-parent families have compared traditional families where the mother takes the load with families where the father takes primary responsibility for childcare.[16] What is clear is that having a highly involved father is not bad for children. If anything, the effects are positive. In addition to a better relationship with their father, children raised in this way have been found to be more independent, to see themselves as more in control of what happens to them, to have greater intellectual ability, and to be more accepting of non-traditional family roles. Contrary to popular assumption the boys are no less masculine, and the girls no less feminine, than the boys and girls from more traditional homes.

Thus the findings of these studies suggest that children benefit from having a highly involved father, and that fathers play a part in children's development of independence and intellectual skills. But it may be the presence of a second highly involved parent rather than the sex of that parent that has the positive effect. Remember also that mothers in families with highly involved fathers are likely to feel more satisfied with their lives and so family relationships in general may be more harmonious. As Michael Lamb has pointed out, in all of these studies the fathers were highly involved with their children because both parents wanted it that way.[2] The picture is quite different when fathers are forced into this role, often because they become unemployed while the mother still has a job. Under these circumstances the outcomes for children are not good. What seems to matter is not how much fathers are involved with their children but how they feel about it. For positive outcomes, it is both parents wanting the father to be responsible for bringing up the children that seems to be the key.

> 'We have a daughter of 12 and a son who is 18 and I suppose my son is closer to me and my daughter is closer to her mother. I don't think that's purely because of gender. My wife worked away a lot so in a sense I was the major parent for my son. She was often away for weeks at a time because of her job. That meant I spent a lot of time with my son as the main parent and that has probably meant that I have a closer relationship with him. My wife changed jobs after my daughter was born and then spent more time with my daughter. So when he was her age I probably did more with him than I do with her now.'

Another way of examining the influence of fathers is to study traditional two-parent families to see whether different types of fathers have different effects on their children. We have already seen from Martha Cox's research that men who spend time and enjoy being with their infants have a more secure relationship with them by the time they are a year old. Other studies have found the same. But it is not just the child's relationship with the father that is improved by the father's involvement; relationships with other children are better as well. In a study of pre-schoolers, those who were securely attached to their father at a year old were found to play more harmoniously with their peers.[17] When Lise Youngblade and Jay Belsky followed up children from age 3 to age 5, they found that those who had a good relationship with their father at 3 years old had better friendships when they were 5.[18] Studies of school-age children have produced similar findings. The National Survey of Families and Households, conducted in the United States, has shown that fathers who are actively involved with their 5- to 18-year-old children have sons and daughters with fewer emotional and behavioural problems and who are more likely to get along well with others and do as their parents ask.[19] And it seems that it is not only children's social development that is improved by involvement with the father; children benefit intellectually as well. In a study that followed up 1-year-old children until the age of 7, those who had a positive relationship with their father were found to have higher IQ scores and to do better when they entered school.[20]

Although these studies indicate that having a warm and involved father is beneficial to children's social development, it is possible that children who have good relationships with their father are more sociable in general (which may have caused him to be more involved with them in the first place!), and may well have had better friendships with other children whether or not they got on well with their dad. The most likely explanation is a mixture of the two; there are benefits for children of having a close relationship with their father, but whether or not they have a close relationship with him will depend, to some extent at least, on how responsive and sociable they are themselves.

Does 'maleness' matter?

'He's a great kid. He's my best pal.'

Although fathers spend much less time with their children than do mothers, it seems that they can play an important role in their children's lives. How long fathers spend with their children seems to matter less than what they do when they are with them. The more that fathers are actively involved in parenting, the better the outcome for children's social and emotional development. But it does not seem to be their maleness that matters. If their gender was important we would expect children without fathers, and children with highly involved fathers, to differ in terms of their masculinity and femininity from children in traditional two-parent families. There is no evidence that this is true. Instead, it seems that fathers have a positive effect on their children's development in the same way as do mothers. Fathers who are affectionate to their children, who are sensitive to their needs, and who respond appropriately to their emotions, are more likely than distant fathers to have well-adjusted children. So it appears that it is their role as an additional parent, not as a male parent, that is beneficial for the child. There is, however, one aspect of fathers' behaviour that is special to them – their greater involvement in lively play. Whereas mothers spend much of their time in day-to-day caretaking, it is often through play that fathers and children build their relationship. Whether or not the way in which fathers play with their children makes a contribution to children's development that is distinct from that of mothers' remains uncertain. What is certain, however, is that from the point of view of children, fathers make great playmates.

Chapter 3

Genetic ties

Related or not?

The old saying 'Blood runs thicker than water' is familiar to us all and reflects a deep-seated belief that genetic bonds are stronger than even the closest of friendships. But what truth does this adage hold when it comes to parents and their children? Is it better for children to be genetically related to their parents, and if so, is it the genetic link itself, or something else, that makes the difference? These questions will be explored by looking at families with children who lack a genetic link with one or both parents: adoptive families, donor insemination families, egg donation families, families created through surrogacy and, finally, stepfamilies.

Adoption

There is no doubt that adopted children fare better through childhood and adult life than children who are raised in institutions, or by parents who do not want them. But adoptive families are different from natural families in a number of important ways that may affect the relationship between the parents and the child. The obvious difference is that children in adoptive families are genetically unrelated to their parents, but other differences exist as well. These mothers and fathers have often experienced years of infertility treatment before becoming parents, followed by further lengthy investigations of their suitability to adopt. All of this can put a strain on their relationship and take its toll on their emotional state. When they finally announce to their family and friends that they plan to adopt a child, the reaction is often less than enthusiastic. If not greeted with outright disapproval, the response, at best, may be one of disappointment and regret.

> 'When she knew that we were having problems getting pregnant she said to my husband "Now if you ever say to me you're going to adopt, never ever expect me to think of them as my grandchildren".'

But once they arrive, adopted babies are usually greeted warmly. For the adoptive parents themselves, the baby marks the end of what, for many, has been a long period of distress and despair. It is perhaps not surprising then, that in spite of their difficulties in becoming parents, adoptive mothers and fathers cope with the transition to family life very well. In fact, a study that compared pregnant couples with couples who were expecting to adopt found that pregnant women were more likely to feel depressed than adoptive mothers-to-be; and four months after the baby's arrival, the adoptive parents were coping better with the physical demands of parenthood and found family life more enjoyable.[1] Research has also shown that adopted infants are just as securely attached to their mother when they are a year old as are naturally conceived infants.[2]

It is not until the infant becomes a toddler that parents face the first real challenge of adoptive family life – telling their child about the adoption. Social workers always encourage parents to be open with their children, and these days most parents follow their advice.

'When you go through the adoption process, and you speak to the social workers, that's what they suggest you do, and I would never think of doing anything else.'

'It's something the social workers made very clear, and we agreed with them. The child's bound to find out sooner or later, and if it's later I think it could be a tremendous shock to them.'

It is now generally accepted that knowledge about their origins helps adopted children to develop a secure sense of identity.[3] Secrecy, on the other hand, can interfere with family relationships and, as a result, harm the psychological well-being not only of the child but also of the future adult. And those who find out about their adoption by accident, through someone else, or during a difficult period in their lives are likely to feel particularly distressed.

'I didn't want her to grow up as if she's been living some sort of lie. I didn't want anything like that. I just wanted to tell her the truth right from the word go. She has a little book. She reads about "Jane is adopted". She reads it all the time.'

'It never seemed to me that there was any choice whatsoever about telling him. I think if you turn it into a secret it would become something furtive and potentially shocking. I mean, if you have a big telling session when they're teenagers you build it up into a big deal that way.'

'I felt that if he suddenly found out at 14 say, or something like that, that he was adopted it would be much harder than if he knew all along. He'd think we'd lied to him and then he'd wonder what else we'd kept from him.'

Another reason for openness is that, because there was no pregnancy, others know about the adoption and may tell the child.

'Well obviously most of our neighbours know because one day we came home with this little bundle. A lady I often talk to, she came up and said "Oh she's lovely who's baby is she?" and I said "She's mine" and she sort of looked as if to say "Hang on a minute I don't remember you being pregnant". So, of course, it came out then, I said, "We're adopting her" so it came out like that.'

'One reason we told her is that my friends all knew, and at the time we got her a lot of them had children so they knew she was adopted, and it was obvious it could come out in conversation at some point.'

It is not easy for parents to tell their children that they are adopted. From that point on, their children know that they have other parents as well. Adoptive parents worry that the child's feelings towards them will change. They also worry about the distress that knowledge about the adoption may bring to the child, and about the possible damaging effects to the child's sense of security and self-esteem. Once parents disclose to their children that they are adopted, they can no longer pretend that their relationship with their children is exactly the same as that of biological parents.

Most parents begin to tell their children that they are adopted when they are between 2 and 4 years old.

'The social worker said the best thing to do was to tell her early, and I always had this horror in my mind that someone might tell her at school – and I never ever wanted that to happen.'

'I think if it's done right from birth, it becomes just a way of life for them. It's their life, it's nothing unusual. But if you sit them down when they're 5 or something and say "Right, we're going to tell you something dear!" then it becomes something really big. With this way it's just their life.'

'Her friend's mother has just had a baby and of course she is all excited about that. She saw this lady getting bigger and bigger and then the baby came. She just asked "Mummy did I come out of your tummy?" It was on a Saturday morning in the bathroom, so I thought "Right, now's the time".'

To help them understand, parents usually tell young children stories about their adoption, or stories of other children being adopted.

'As soon as he was old enough to speak we started saying the word adopted to him. And then we got a book called *Mr Fairweather and his Family*. It was a nice story about a man who met this lady and they got married and they got a little house, and there's a cat and a dog, and the room. This room was empty, and they longed for a baby but the baby didn't come. So they went along to a home, a children's home, and of course it's a lot easier in the book, and they picked this little baby boy. And, you know, everyone was happy and eventually they picked a little baby girl and there was a family. And we used to read this book to him and he was very happy with this book.'

'She was 4 when we adopted our son so we took the opportunity to get out the photographs and show the first pictures we had of her, and talked to her about going to Court and what it was like when she came. She came with us to Court for the adoption of our son and, in fact, the judge didn't speak to us, he talked to her, asked if she wanted him and I thought "If she says no!" And she thought it was wonderful.'

But just because children have been told about their adoption does not necessarily mean that they understand very much about it. They may say that they are adopted, and may even be able to tell the story of their adoption, but it is not until they reach school age and develop more complex thought processes that they become aware of what adoption really means.[3]

'I don't think Sally really understands fully what it means. She knows that she grew in another lady's tummy, and this lady couldn't look after her, and that Mummy and Daddy adopted her. So that's basically what she'll say.'

'We didn't really tell her as such. Adoption is just a word that has always been used. So she's really just grown up knowing. But knowing, and fully understanding, can be quite different. Although you can say she's been told, that she knows, there's just that moment when understanding sinks in. I mean, it'll still be a shock.'

It is as children reach school age that they begin to ask questions about their biological parents. What do they look like? Where are they now? Will I ever see them again? And why did they have me adopted? The realisation that in order to have been adopted they must have been given up by their biological parents can cause children to feel less positive about being adopted than they ever had before. Feelings of loss, rejection and confusion are common as they become aware of what has happened to them. For parents, coping with their children's negative feelings about adoption can present one of the most difficult challenges of adoptive family life.[3]

'Daniel is quite sensitive and he's questioned it quite a lot. We're getting quite a bit of testing you know. He'll say, maybe if he's been told off and his brother Tom hasn't, "You love Tom more than me" and he needs a lot of reassuring. He knows that's not the case but he needs reassuring all the time.'

'He has on a couple of occasions said to me that I'm not his real mum, which hurt at the time. But I know how to handle it now. I say I am your mum. It was quite a shock the first time. But he admitted afterwards that he said it to hurt me. He said "You hurt me so I was hurting you". This was his way of getting back at me.'

Adolescence can also be a problematic period for adoptive families. It is at this stage that young people develop a sense of identity – a sense of who they are. And to develop a secure identity, young people need to build a coherent story of their lives. Adopted adolescents often become extremely interested in their origins, seeking out information about, and sometimes contact with, their biological parents.[3] Again, for adoptive parents this can be a particularly trying time.

So growing up in an adoptive family can place additional stresses on children that do not exist for those who are raised by their natural parents. But do adopted children function less well as a result? The answer is 'It depends': It depends on a number of factors including the age of the child and, perhaps more importantly, the age at which the child was adopted. Certainly, a higher proportion of adopted children than non-adopted children are seen by mental health professionals. But this does not necessarily mean that adopted children are more likely to have psychological problems. Instead, adoptive parents may be more likely to seek help when their children show emotional or behavioural difficulties, and there is some evidence that this is the case. However, adopted children do appear to show similar kinds of difficulties as each other which suggests that being adopted, in itself, may place children at greater risk. They tend to be referred to clinics because of conduct problems such as aggression, disobedience, defiance and bullying rather than for emotional problems such as anxiety and depression. They are also more likely to show learning difficulties at school.[4]

Studies of adopted children who have been identified through their local community, rather than through a clinic, are more informative about whether adopted children really are more at risk for psychological problems.[3] Interestingly, what such studies show is that during the pre-school years adopted children are no different from non-adopted children. But as they reach school age – the time when they become aware that they have lost a family as well as gained one – a higher incidence of behavioural problems is detected. As children progress through the teenage years these difficulties become less apparent, but whether they disappear completely is not absolutely clear.

So it seems that adopted children are more likely to show behavioural problems than children of natural parents. But this does not mean that all adopted children have problems, only that more adopted children have problems than would be found in a similar group of non-adopted children. Why should this happen? And what is different about the ones who do show problems, and the ones who do not? There is no single answer to this question. A number of factors seem to play a part.[4] First, biological influences may be involved. Mothers who put their children up for adoption are more likely to have been under stress, eaten badly, smoked cigarettes, drunk too much alcohol and taken drugs during pregnancy, all of which can harm the developing child. They are also more likely to have received poor medical care and to have experienced complications during birth, and to have had psychological problems themselves which may have passed a vulnerability on to the child. The way in which adoptive parents communicate to the child about adoption is also important. The best situation seems to be one where children are able to discuss their adoption freely, and feel a sense of security and support when going through difficult times. Parents who either deny that their family is different and discourage discussion about the child's past, or who overly emphasise that the child is adopted and attribute any difficulties shown by the child to his or her biological origins, are those whose children are most likely to experience difficulties as they grow up.

The age at which a child is adopted is also important.[4] Children who are adopted as infants are generally better adjusted than those who are adopted later in childhood. It is not the age itself that matters. The older children are when they are adopted, the more likely they are to have been neglected or abused before joining their adoptive family. They may also have been separated from their biological mother after having developed a close bond with her, and may even have experienced separation from their biological mother, or from others to whom they had become attached, on more than one occasion. Children who enter an adoptive family under these circumstances are more liable to show problems than those who are raised by their adoptive parents from soon after birth.

Another factor to consider is that adoption is generally viewed by the outside world as a second-best route to parenthood, and adopted children are often stigmatised at school. So we must look beyond the family in trying to understand why adopted children sometimes experience difficulties. In 1996, in Britain, a boy was disqualified from a family golf competition on the grounds that he was adopted. It was argued that because he was not a 'blood relation' he was not eligible to play. If adopted children are exposed to attitudes such as this, it is perhaps not surprising that some find it difficult to feel positive about their adoption as they grow up.

In recent years, some experts have argued that adopted children would benefit from remaining in contact with their biological mother. But concern has also been expressed that this would be confusing for children, and would interfere with the development of secure relationships within their adoptive family. The few reports that exist suggest that, for some children at least, contact with the biological mother can help the child to understand the circumstances of the adoption without undermining his or her sense of belonging to the adoptive family. Nevertheless, only a small number of carefully chosen children have been studied so far and it is too early to say exactly what the consequences are for all concerned.[5]

'It didn't bother my son. He said "Oh fine mum", a typical male. But much more thinking goes on in my daughter's brain. About six months ago she was crying and I said "What's the matter?" and she said "I want to see my other Mummy". She couldn't grasp why she had another Mummy, and where she was, and why she couldn't see her. It was hard to cope with her crying and not being able to satisfy what she wanted. It was the hardest thing to say "Look you can't, there's no way that you can". It was hard for her to actually accept that she couldn't.'

Donor insemination

If a woman is able to have children but her husband is infertile, the couple may opt to have a child by donor insemination. With this procedure, the woman is inseminated using semen donated by another man. Although the procedure itself is very simple, involving the transfer of semen to the vagina by syringe, insemination usually takes place at a clinic so that an anonymous donor can be used and characteristics of the donor can be matched to those of the couple who will become the child's parents. Clinics also screen donors very carefully for illnesses that could be passed on to the child, such as AIDS, to ensure that only healthy men are allowed to donate.

Because donor insemination is like adoption in that one parent, the father, has no genetic link with the child, it is often assumed that the experience of parenting a child conceived by donor insemination is similar to parenting an adopted child. But in many aspects, the two are quite different. The child does have a genetic relationship with one parent, the mother. The child is born to the mother, and the child has not been given up by the biological parents. In all of these ways, donor insemination families are more like natural families than adoptive families.

In sharp contrast to the openness of adoptive parents, most donor insemination parents keep the circumstances of conception secret from their child. Almost all children conceived in this way grow up unaware that the person they know as their dad is not their genetic father. Until recently, doctors have advised parents that there is no need to tell the child, and that if the couple have sex on the same day as the insemination there is always the possibility, however improbable, that the child will have been conceived with the father's sperm.

> 'The doctor said that there is a chance that he is ours, and so we've always looked on it that he is ours. We feel that we are his parents right from the start, from the very first day'.

> 'The thing is, the way I look at it, I still had sex with my husband all the way through. So we're not one hundred per cent sure. And why tell him, if you don't know?'

> 'Who ever knows? You know, the same night you do it, and nobody knows.'

Some couples start out with the intention to tell but never quite get round to it.

> 'We said that we would be open about it, and talk about it with the children, and tell everyone. You know, be quite open about it. I suppose we felt we would do. But we never did.'

The main reason for secrecy is to avoid hurting the child. It is feared that knowing the truth would be deeply upsetting.

> 'I think it would ruin their lives. I think it would shatter them, take away their roots. So, no, I don't plan to tell them.'

> 'It could shatter her peace of mind. You know, it could turn her whole world upside down. If I told her, I don't know how she would react.'

There is also the concern that the child might love the parents less and, in particular, reject the father. In adoptive families, both the mother and the father lack a genetic link with the child so their relationship is balanced in that respect which presents less of a problem for telling.

> 'We had to decide from the start whether we would be open about it or whether it would be a secret forever, and we decided to keep it a secret. We were thinking about the children growing up and, knowing that my husband wasn't their natural father, whether they would feel any differently towards him. We decided we didn't want that, and in their eyes he is their natural father.'

> 'I don't want to ruin the relationship he has with his dad. I think it would be a gamble. They have such a good relationship just now, I would hate to jeopardise it.'

> 'She's got a very happy life and I suppose I worry about how she would react. My husband fears that she might not love him as much as she does now.'

In some families mothers are more inclined towards disclosure than fathers, but respect the father's wishes not to tell.

> 'I can see my husband's point of view. He doesn't want her not to love him. I know it wouldn't make any difference. But he really feels that he doesn't want her to know, because he doesn't want her to change her feelings towards him.'

> 'I couldn't have had her if my husband hadn't signed the forms. That's the way I look at it.'

> 'I think it's a hard enough thing for my husband to bear already without anyone knowing that it's his infertility.'

A major question facing parents is when to tell the child. The time never seems to be quite right. Parents of toddlers often think the child is too young to understand.

'She'd have to be a lot older. I wouldn't tell her before school age. It'd be when she's older and can understand and accept things. I mean she's very good at understanding and accepting things now, but then, being a child she could say "Well, you're not my dad" or something like that. She'd have to be grown up. And then I'd choose my words very carefully.'

But by school age many parents feel it is too late.

'It's too late now really. She's nearly 6. And to shatter the illusion that she's got, I think that would be a bit too much for her.'

'I think we've left it too late. I think if you're going to tell them, you have to do it when they are very young. It's too late now she's 7. I can't think how she'd react. There's no way I could tell her now.'

'I don't know at what stage you'd tell them. They couldn't understand it when they were small. If you told them when they were 11 or 12, I think it could cause real problems for them as they have difficulties with their own sexuality then. Maybe you'd tell them when they're 20 or something, but by that stage it could come as a terrible shock.'

'People make deathbed confessions. But he would be a young man and he wouldn't know where he was and he would lose his identity, wouldn't he?'

There is also the problem of what to tell the child. Unlike adoption, the child needs some knowledge of the facts of life in order to understand donor insemination. And explaining about donor insemination means disclosing that the father is infertile. Although adopted children are told that their parents were unable to have a baby, neither needs to be identified as the infertile partner.

'I think it's quite a hard treatment for a child to understand really. I don't know how I would even begin to explain it. It's quite hard to explain that you've had somebody else's sperm to fertilise your egg, and it's not Daddy's.'

More importantly, when the donor is anonymous, as is usually the case, parents have little information to give the child about the genetic father, so they are unable to respond to the child's inevitable questions about who their genetic father is, and what he is like. This situation contrasts sharply with that of adoptive parents who usually have detailed information about the child's parents and often photographs as well.

'When we first knew we were going to do it, we were going to be open with everyone, and tell the children, and not have any secrets. But it's not worked out that way at all! We haven't told anybody. We've talked about it and we feel that if we tell the children it will cause more problems than not telling because they might want to find out more about it and they won't be able to. And they might worry about it.'

'The way it stands, if I do tell him that biologically he's not his father's, there's no more he can gain from it because he's never going to find out who his biological father is.'

'I think it could create problems, rather than making it easier for them. Because unlike adopted children, they've got no way of finding out anything about their genetic father, and I know of people who've been adopted who do want to try and contact their natural parents because they feel they want to know something about them. So I think that if they wanted to find out something and couldn't, then you'd have held out the prospect of something and then denied it to them. In a way I feel they should be told, but I can't see that it's right to tell them when they can't follow it up.'

Whereas some parents decide against telling their children because of these difficulties, others feel that there is simply no need to tell.

'We just feel that she's ours. It's like it was done, but it's forgotten about. From the day I conceived, it was just like she was my husband's. She's never been thought of as anything else.'

'I don't feel any need to. I don't feel that they're not our children.'

'If you are adopted then you are given away by somebody, for whatever reason, and if you're told you are adopted and you want to contact your mother or father so that they can stave off any feelings of rejection then that can add to what you've got. But I think that when it's only to do with a cell then that's our business. All you concentrate on is the fact that they're a completely unique individual.'

Those who believe there is no need to tell often emphasise social rather than biological aspects of parenting.

'He was there, right from the very moment of conception. He is their father in every true sense of the word. He was there at their delivery, and has been there through all their ups and downs. He is their dad.'

'We just never considered it because as far as my husband was concerned he may not clinically be his dad, but he was his dad! And it was just as simple as that. There was no reason to tell him.'

'I think that parenthood is what you do. It's how you are with them. It's the work that goes into it rather than the actual conception. It's the everyday nitty gritty.'

Some couples undergoing donor insemination tell members of their family, or friends, while they are having treatment. Telling others can provide a source of support.

'I couldn't trust anybody like I trust my mum never to mention it, or say anything. And she never has. She's never once said anything, right from when I first told her what I intended to do. I couldn't quite put my trust in anybody else, not like I could with my mum.'

'I told someone at work. I did actually find it quite a help that there was someone I could talk to. It's something I can't really talk about at all, even now. It's unmentioned really.'

However, not everyone can be trusted to keep confidences. Telling even one person means that there will always be a risk of the child finding out. It only takes one person, one casual remark, for the truth to be known. And when this happens, it is often at the worst possible time for the child – during an argument, or when the parents divorce, or when a mother or father dies.

'I feel that by telling my sister, she'd have to share it with her husband, and I couldn't trust her husband not to say anything, so we always felt that with the less people who knew, the less chance of anything being said. I mean people do get angry, and they do say spiteful things.'

'Well, we got into a bit of a state. We'd told my mother, and she blabbed to my aunt, and my aunt assumed that my older daughter knew, and last year when she was here she was talking to my older daughter about things and told her. She didn't realise she didn't know. At the time, you feel you want to tell someone because you are under quite a lot of stress. I wish I hadn't, of course, because it caused a lot of trouble – a lot of trouble. Now we shall have to tell her because her sister knows. We couldn't let her go through life not knowing something that her sister knows.'

'There's only one thing I wish I hadn't done. I wish I hadn't told any of my friends. I told a few friends in – well, not secrecy – but thinking that they wouldn't go and pass it on. And they went and told their mothers. I've bumped into the mothers and, especially when my daughter was younger, they would say 'Oh she really looks like your husband'. And I knew what they were saying. She did look like my husband when she was younger, but I think they were just trying to make me feel better. But they weren't really because once they found out it escalated. In the end, so many people knew. All I was worried about then was would it get back to my daughter eventually, you know, later on? I was worried that, in future years, they might be sitting talking, and their children might hear, and they might go to her and tell her what they had overheard.'

Over the years, concern has grown about the possible negative effects of keeping the child's origin secret,[6] particularly the potential damage to family relationships and, consequently, to the emotional well-being of the child. We know that adopted children benefit from knowing about their biological parents, and for this reason it is increasingly being argued that children conceived by donor insemination should also be told about the circumstances of their birth. Some would even go as far as telling the child who the donor is. Although anonymity is preferred in most countries, in Sweden children can find out who their genetic father is when they are 18 years old, and in New Zealand many clinics advise parents to be open with their children and recruit donors who are willing to be identified to their offspring in the future. One reason for not identifying the donor is that fewer men would offer to donate if there was a possibility that, at some time in the future, a stranger would knock on their door claiming to be their child. In a survey of donors carried out in the UK in 1993 to 1994 it was found that two-thirds of donors would not have volunteered if children resulting from their donation had been able to find them.[7]

Those in favour of telling children point to the potential harm secrecy may do to family relationships. As one psychologist put it, secrets 'separate those who know (the parents) from those who do not (the child)'.[8] Children can often sense when they are not being told something because a taboo surrounds the discussion of certain topics; parents often give themselves away by their tone of voice, facial expression or body posture, or by abruptly changing the subject. It is not known whether children conceived by donor insemination become aware that a secret about their parentage is being kept from them, but they might become suspicious if their parents always change the topic of conversation whenever the subject of who they look like crops up. Family secrets can jeopardise communication between family members, cause tension and result in a distancing of some members of the family from others.

Partly due to the secrecy surrounding donor insemination, there is little research on these parents and their children, so we do not know a great deal about how families are affected by being created in this way. In the largest study, carried out in Spain, Italy, the Netherlands and the UK, 111 families with a child conceived by donor insemination were compared with 116 families with a child conceived by in vitro fertilisation (IVF) (where the child was genetically related to both parents), 115 adoptive families (where the child was adopted in infancy) and 120 families with a naturally conceived child.[9] IVF, or 'test-tube' babies are conceived by fertilising the mother's egg with the father's sperm in the laboratory, and transferring the resulting embryo to the mother's womb. All the children were between 4 and 8 years old. Detailed information was obtained by interview and questionnaire about the mother's relationship with the child, the father's relationship with the child, and the child's social and emotional development, and teachers reported on the child's behaviour at school. The children themselves took part in an assessment of their self-esteem and their perceptions of their relationship with their parents.

It was striking that not one set of donor insemination parents had told their child that their father was genetically unrelated to them and that they had been conceived using the sperm of an anonymous donor. Moreover, most parents had made the decision never to tell. In Italy, all the parents said that they would always keep this information secret, and this was also the case for the large majority of parents in the other countries. But in spite of the concerns that have been expressed about the possible harm that secrecy might do to family relationships, donor insemination parents were found to be closer to their children, and interacted with them more on a day-to-day basis, than did natural parents. This was true of fathers as well as mothers. It was not that the natural parents were neglectful or uncaring but, instead, the donor insemination parents were particularly involved. It seems that couples who go to great lengths to become parents are very committed when a longed-for child eventually arrives. Interestingly, the donor insemination and the IVF mothers and fathers were very alike as parents. This shows that when children are wanted very much, the absence of a genetic link between the child and the father does not harm the relationship between either parent and the child. Similarly, the adoptive parents were more like the parents who had received assisted reproduction (donor insemination or IVF) than the parents of a naturally conceived child.

What about the children themselves? Donor insemination children were generally found to be doing well and did not show signs of psychological problems. But in spite of their highly committed parents, donor insemination children were no better adjusted, and did not see themselves as having a closer relationship with their mother or father than the naturally conceived children. It seems that above a certain level of parental warmth and involvement, even greater input from parents makes little difference to the well-being of their child.

Does this mean that the absence of a genetic link between a father and his child makes no difference to the adjustment of the child? It seems so, but it is too early to be sure. It is important to remember that the oldest children studied were only 8 years old, and not one of them had been told that he or she had been conceived using the sperm of an anonymous donor. It remains to be seen what happens to these children as they grow up, both those who are told and those who are not, particularly as they reach adolescence. This is the time when children become concerned with issues of identity, and begin to have more difficult relationships with their parents. It is also a time when adopted children show a greater incidence of behavioural problems – accompanied by a greater interest in their biological parents.

At present, all that is known about the consequences for children conceived by donor insemination of being told that the person they know of as their father is not their genetic parent comes from anecdotal reports of adults who have found out about the circumstances of their birth. The general view is that they would have preferred to be told at an early age. In fact, some reported feeling deceived by their parents and angry with them, and believed that they lacked a clear sense of who they were as a result of their upbringing. Because these adults are not a representative sample of individuals conceived by donor insemination, it is difficult to know how much their experiences are common to others with the same background. Many questions remain unanswered. Do children who are not told about the circumstances of their birth sense that something is amiss in their lives? Do children who are told feel disturbed by this knowledge? And do they have a strong desire for information about, or contact with, their genetic father? Only systematic studies of those who have been told and those who have not will shed light on the effects of donor insemination on childhood and adult lives.

Egg donation

Egg donation is like donor insemination in that the child is genetically related to only one parent, but in this case it is the mother and not the father with whom there is no genetic link. Egg donation is a much more complex procedure than donor insemination, involving the IVF technique of fertilising the donor's egg with the father's sperm in the laboratory, followed by the transfer of the embryo to the mother's womb. Women who donate eggs must take medication, undergo a series of ultrasound scans and have the eggs surgically removed from their ovary – a rather more intrusive and unpleasant experience than that of men who donate semen. It is only since 1983 that it has been possible for women to conceive a child using a donated egg, and thus for children to be born to mothers with whom they have no genetic link.[10]

'The way we look at it, if my wife hadn't fed and nurtured our daughter in her body, that child wouldn't be here. So 99.9 per cent recurring, she is our child.'

The concerns that have been expressed about egg donation are similar to those raised by donor insemination. Again, it is the effect of secrecy about the child's conception that has been the topic of greatest debate. But unlike donor insemination where the donor is usually anonymous, egg donors are more often relatives or friends of the parents and may remain in contact with the family as the child grows up.

'My friend was aware that we'd been trying to have a baby for years. She'd always lent a willing ear to listen to my problems. I'd said to her that it looked like our best chance was with donated eggs, and she just offered. I wasn't fishing. It hadn't occurred to me at all. It was completely out of the blue. She talked it over with her husband, and I talked it over with my husband, and we all talked it over together. And it didn't appear to be a problem. Because of distance we only see her a few times a year. Our son sees her too. My friend feels that he is my child. She has told me that she doesn't feel anything more than that.'

Because egg donation is a relatively new procedure, little is known about the consequences for children of being conceived in this way. One small study of families with 3- to 8-year-old children has compared egg donation families with both donor insemination families and families with a genetically related child conceived by *in vitro* fertilisation (involving similar procedures to egg donation but using the mother's egg).[11] On the whole the three groups of families were functioning well and did not differ from each other in terms of the quality of parenting or the child's psychological well-being. Where differences did exist, they reflected even more positive relationships in egg donation families. This was particularly true for parents' reports of stress associated with parenting, which was lowest for parents of an egg donation child. However, most of the children studied had been conceived using the egg of an anonymous donor. What is not known is the effect on the child of being conceived with the egg of a known donor – a relative or family friend – who continues to play a part in family life.

Some couples for whom both partners are infertile have given birth to a child conceived using donated sperm as well as a donated egg. Under these circumstances the egg and sperm are fertilised in the laboratory and the resulting embryo is returned to the mother's womb. The child is therefore like an adopted child in that he or she has no genetic link with either parent, and for this reason the procedure is sometimes referred to as 'prenatal adoption'. The difference is that the parents experience pregnancy and the child's birth. No studies of the development of children conceived by embryo donation have yet been carried out. As with donor insemination and egg donation, concern has been expressed that the children will be at risk for psychological problems arising from uncertainty about their identity as they grow up.

Surrogacy

Of all the different ways in which families can be created today, it is the practice of surrogacy where a woman bears a child for another woman that is the most controversial. There are two types of surrogacy: partial surrogacy where conception occurs using the commissioning father's sperm and the surrogate mother's egg (the surrogate mother may attend a clinic to be inseminated or may inseminate herself at home), and full surrogacy where both the egg and the sperm come from the commissioning parents (this has to be carried out at a clinic). Thus children born through partial surrogacy are like egg donation children in that they are genetically related to their father but not to their mother, and children born through full surrogacy are genetically related to both of their parents. It is also possible, although less common, for surrogacy to take place using donated eggs and/or sperm.

A major concern about surrogacy is the potential for exploitation of the surrogate mother.[12] Sisters or friends of infertile women may be coerced into hosting a pregnancy, or women in need of money may become surrogate mothers because of financial hardship, without awareness of the consequences for their own or their families' lives. Relinquishing a child after nine months of pregnancy can be much more difficult than anticipated at the start, and can leave the surrogate mother feeling rejected, lonely and depressed. Problems can also arise when the surrogate mother decides to keep the child, a situation that can be deeply distressing for everyone concerned. This was recently highlighted in the UK when the relationship broke down between a surrogate mother and the commissioning parents, and the surrogate mother decided not to give up the baby. She announced that she had obtained an abortion, only to admit a few days later that this was untrue and that she planned to keep the child.

There is no research on children born through surrogacy. Although there are similarities with children in adoptive and assisted reproduction families, children born through surrogacy differ in ways that may be detrimental to their emotional well-being as they grow up. It is not known, for example, how a child will feel about having been created for the purpose of being given away to other parents, particularly when the surrogate mother was paid to host the pregnancy. Or, if the surrogate mother remains in contact with the family, what the impact of two mothers will be on his or her social, emotional and identity development through childhood and into adult life, especially in families where the surrogate mother is also the genetic mother of the child. Although it might be expected that contact with the surrogate mother would be a positive experience for children in that they could develop a clear understanding of their origins, the involvement of the surrogate mother may have a negative effect on the commissioning couple's relationship, and on the woman's security in her mothering role, particularly when the surrogate mother and the commissioning father are the genetic parents of the child.

Stepfamilies

Children in stepfamilies are also raised by a parent with whom they have no genetic link. However, unlike most adopted children, or children conceived by egg or sperm donation or by partial surrogacy, many of these children grow up with their genetic parents in their early years, or with one genetic parent alone, before moving into a stepfamily. Not only do they need to adapt to life with a stepparent, but many also lose close contact with a biological parent with whom they had once shared their daily lives. It has been estimated that about 25 per cent of children will find themselves in a stepfamily before they are adults, and some will be raised in more than one stepfamily during their childhood years.[13]

We know from fairy-tales that step-parents are not the most popular of people. Just think of Cinderella, or Snow White, or Hansel and Gretel, all treated cruelly by their wicked stepmothers. But is this an accurate portrayal? Are stepmothers really as nasty as they seem? In fact, many more children have a stepfather than a stepmother because most children remain with their mother when their parents divorce, and for this reason research has tended to focus on stepfather rather than stepmother families.

The most notable research on stepfamilies has been carried out by Mavis Hetherington and her colleagues in the United States. As part of her study of 4-year-old children whose parents had divorced (discussed in Chapter 1), the researchers followed up the children whose mother had remarried by the time they were aged 10.[13,14] What they found was that the outcome was different for boys and girls. Girls were much happier when their mother remained unmarried. Any adjustment problems that they had developed around the time of the divorce had usually disappeared and they generally had a close relationship with their mother. It was those whose mother had remarried who were experiencing problems, particularly in their relationship with their stepfather whom many found difficult to accept. Their behaviour did improve as time went on, but even two years after their mother's remarriage they still tended to be antagonistic towards both their mother and their stepfather.

> 'Before she got married we were very close. We were like sisters really. When she got married we drifted apart. You see I was in the same bedroom with my mum until I was 16, so we were close. And then suddenly, it was like he's invading my territory because he's going to my mum's room and I felt shut out a bit. Although I was happy for her to have found somebody, I still felt he's not my father and there's times when I sort of resented him, and thought there's no way I'll call him dad. And there's no way I'd call him dad to this day, because he's not my father. My stepdad and me, we didn't really get on that well, because it was like he's not my father, you know, he's just a man that's come into my mum's life.'

In contrast, boys whose mothers remarried showed fewer problems than those whose mothers had not married again and, providing their stepfather was supportive, had developed a relationship with him that was positive in at least some respects.

> 'He was alright because he was interested in us as well. It wasn't just my mum he took an interest in. He used to take us out. It just clicked. We got on ever so well. He was a bit difficult after they got married, a bit stricter. That was hard to adjust to, how we'd been with mum and then a man coming into the relationship, and I found it hard. But it worked out after a while. He was always

there. If you wanted him he was there. That meant more to me than anything, him just being there all the time.'

'At the beginning I was pleased in a certain way that I now had a father as it were. Because all my other friends had dads and they'd take them out and buy them presents and give them love and I thought that was what I was going to get, that I hadn't as a child. But in another way I suppose I was a bit jealous that somebody had actually come in and disturbed the relationship that me and my mum had at the time. I think I must have been very naughty, you know, been very jealous and come in at the wrong moments and saying things and having tempers and stuff like that. But that wears off as you realise that this person is going to stay.'

When their mother remarries, children do not just gain a stepfather. They often find themselves with stepbrothers and sisters as well.

'I was jealous of the fact that he had a son and he used to come home for Christmas and every other weekend. And although it was like I had a brother, it was great you know we could talk and that, but he had a sense of superiority because he had an actual dad. He used to get more attention and I used to notice this. I used to notice it with bigger presents at Christmas. He used to give more attention to Charlie. There wasn't the same companionship between my stepdad and me.'

The stepfathers who developed the best relationships with their stepchildren were warm and supportive at first without being controlling, and then gradually began to exert discipline as time went on.

'I suppose that the good thing about my stepdad coming into our lives was that he always kept order. He used to pin me down a bit, keep me under control, so that I wouldn't be like the other kids in my class, out of control and wild. He always was very stern. But I think that he's helped me. He was very tough on wanting me to learn all the time, and doing times tables, and reading. He'd say "You've got to do this, and not sit in front of the television". I'd come home from school and have to do homework and he'd mark it. And when you're little you don't want to, it's part of growing up.'

In a later study the same researchers looked at older children, examining the effects of moving into a stepfamily on children who were approaching adolescence at the time their mother remarried.[15] Unlike the younger children of the earlier study, these older children did not adapt at all well to their new family circumstances. Their behaviour was often disruptive and demanding and their relationship with their stepfather was characterised by hostility and resentment on the part of the child and, after many unsuccessful attempts to form a positive relationship, disengagement on the part of the stepfather. Even more discouraging was the finding that no improvement took place in the child's behaviour in general, and towards the stepfather in particular, over the course of the next two years. By this time many stepfathers had stopped trying to form a close relationship and exerted little discipline or control over their stepchildren's behaviour. It seemed that in the end they just gave up.

'She got remarried when I was about 9 or 10. But I hated him. And me and Chris, that's my stepdad, we used to have some terrible fights, we really did.'

'There were always arguments with me and my brothers every day. But just normal things like clean up your mess, and I'd be like, you know, no chance. He tried to be a father-figure, but we wore him down, you know, I'm telling you we did.'

'I remember going round to people's houses after school, and there always used to be, you know, the dad. And I used to notice that things were different. And though I had a stepdad now, he's just like a ghost. I could see with the other fathers they were giving more time to their children, and they would pick them up and take them out. I'm not saying my stepdad didn't care for me, but it was in a way that because he's come into this family he's got to give support. He's got to do this because that's the contract as it were.'

Thus it appears that when children enter stepfamilies early in childhood they can settle into their new circumstances quite well, and this is especially true of sons. But when children make this transition during their early adolescent years there is much less chance that the stepfather will ever be accepted by either daughters or sons.

'He's never really said anything bad to me. He's had a few words with me, maybe if I've been cheeky to my mum. But then I've said "What are you talking to me like that for? You're not my dad."'

Although less is known about stepmother than stepfather families, the research that does exist suggests that children have even greater difficulty in adjusting to a stepmother than to a stepfather, and that conflict with stepmothers is more common among daughters than among sons.[16] But the findings are not all negative. There are indications that adolescent girls get on better with their stepmothers as time goes on, alongside an improvement in their psychological adjustment. Stepmothers are thought to be more difficult to accept than step-fathers because women are generally more involved in the day-to-day care of children than are fathers, which places greater strain on their relationship with stepchildren.

A recent large-scale longitudinal survey in the Avon area of Great Britain has given Judy Dunn and her colleagues the opportunity to look at not just the consequences for children of growing up in stepfamilies but also to explore in detail why some children are badly affected and others are not.[17] What the researchers found, based on information from 8,000 4-year-olds, was that the children's psychological problems had more to do with their social circumstances including their mother being depressed, poor relationships with their mother and father, and economic hardship, than the fact that they lived in a stepfamily. A more in-depth examination of 190 of these families showed that whether a child is the parent's own biological child or a stepchild clearly makes a difference; parents are more affectionate towards, and more supportive of, their own biological children than their stepchildren.

Is blood thicker than water?

In this chapter we have considered the psychological consequences for children of being genetically unrelated to their father (when conceived by donor insemination or raised with a stepfather), to their mother (when conceived by egg donation, raised by a stepmother or conceived by partial surrogacy) and to both parents (when adopted or conceived by egg *and* sperm (embryo) donation). Studies of adoption and step-parenting have shown that the lack of genetic relatedness between a child and one or both parents is associated with behavioural problems in the child. But not all children in adoptive or stepfamilies experience problems. This depends on many factors including their age, as well as the age at which the transition to their new family took place, and also on how parents handle the new family situation. So it seems that it is not the absence of a genetic relationship, in itself, that is problematic.

Children born through egg and/or sperm donation do not experience the loss of an existing parent; nor do they need to negotiate relationships with new family members. Research on children conceived by gamete donation shows not only that these children are functioning well, but also that they have more involved parents than children who have been naturally conceived. This tells us that a genetic link appears to be less important for positive family functioning than a strong commitment to parenthood. One father who has both genetically related and genetically unrelated children put it like this:

> 'I have six children, some are adopted and some are naturally born. And I think I can truly say, cross my heart and hope to die, that I do not feel differently to any of them, and regard all six of them as being my children. I've asked myself time and time again, if I was on a sinking ship – well, I do happen to sail so it's relevant – if the boat was sinking, would I show a preference for my naturally born child versus my adopted child? And the answer is, most certainly, no I would not.'

What we do not yet know about families created by assisted reproduction or by surrogacy, however, is whether certain characteristics of these families such as secrecy about the child's origins, or contact between the child and a known egg or sperm donor or surrogate mother, will have a good, bad or indifferent influence on the child as he or she grows up.

Chapter 4

Parents' sexual orientation
Heterosexual or homosexual?

'I didn't understand then, I was only little, about 5 years old, and my mum and Sarah sleeping together didn't mean anything to me. My dad was very understanding really. After they split up I was forever saying to my mum do you think you and dad will get back together? And I used to go and see my dad and say don't you want to get back together with mum? And then he just sat me down and explained that it was my mum's way of living and that is up to her. He didn't hate her or anything. And I thought that was brilliant.'

This girl's parents were 19 years old when they married and had known each other for two years. Although her mother had first been attracted to girls at school when she was 14 years old, she felt that marriage was what was expected of her and had a reasonably happy relationship with her husband for the best part of thirteen years. She had experienced a few casual lesbian encounters in the past, but it was meeting Sarah, and falling in love with her, that was the turning point in her life. Only then did she realise how fulfilling a relationship could be, and at the age of 32 she left her husband and set up home with her daughter, Sarah and Sarah's 3-year-old daughter Kate. Looking back, she sees her decision to marry as a mistake, and being uprooted from her family home as the unhappiest experience of her life.

This story is not unusual. For many lesbian women, particularly in the past, the pressure to marry has been so strong that feelings of attraction to other women have been pushed aside in an attempt to conform. In some cases these feelings have not even been recognised as such until a close friendship has unexpectedly blossomed into a love affair.

The breakup of their parents' marriage can be devastating for children, and the introduction of a step-parent can be fraught with tension and hostility. But children in lesbian families sometimes find it easier to accept their mother's new female partner than children of heterosexual mothers can accept a new male partner. The female partner is often viewed as an additional parent rather than as a substitute for their absent father, and many children continue to have a close relationship with their father as well.

In some cases, the child's relationship with the mother's partner is closer than with his or her father:

> 'My mum and dad separated when I was 3. My father wasn't a very good person with children anyway. He didn't like children much and so I didn't have an awful lot to do with him. The only time he would take an interest in us is if we were all dressed up to go somewhere and he would say 'These are my children'. If we were dirty, he wouldn't want to know. I don't really remember him. The first person I really remember is Julie who's my mother's partner. As far as I'm concerned Julie is my other parent. You know, I don't feel any less wanted because Julie isn't my father. Instead, I feel that Julie would never have stayed if she didn't love us. My mother is definitely my mum, there's no question about it. But I love Julie as much, in a different way. I love her for her merits. She's not my biological parent so I love her for herself because she is special. My dad just lives up the road. Sometimes I bump into him at the supermarket and say hello. If you saw us in the street you'd think we were just neighbours. He's not the sort of person who I could feel had let me down because he never did anything for me.'

For young children, the realisation that their family is different dawns gradually. This girl's parents separated when she was 3 years old, and she was then brought up by her mother and her mother's partner:

> 'I always knew that they slept in the same bed and did the sort of things that men and women do. I don't think I thought about the sex side of it until I was a teenager. I must have sorted it out in my head. When I did get to the awareness stage it didn't worry me.'

This boy was at junior school when his parents divorced and his mother's partner came to live with him:

> 'At the time I hadn't really thought very much about their relationship and about how physical it was or wasn't. I remember mum explaining that their relationship was like a man and woman, and that they would like to get married but couldn't because they were both ladies. To a 10-year-old that meant that they lived together in a house and they cooked dinner together. That was as much as I understood about their relationship at that point. It was quite a long time before I realised that their relationship was unusual. When I first realised I think that it was a bit of a shock, even although I had been living with it all these years. I'd accepted it as normal and never thought of it as anything unusual.'

The same was true for this girl who was also at junior school when her mother's partner moved into the family home. Her parents had divorced before she started school:

'I didn't see it as a sexual relationship. She was just somebody who was around a lot. Who was fun to be with. And she made mum happy. I can't think of a day when the knowledge hit me. As early as I can remember there were women in my mum's life rather than men. It was like a gradual dawning. In school we'd be talking about "lezzies" but I didn't connect it. I had inklings but I didn't particularly want to think about it. And by 13 or 14 I sort of accepted it.'

Although children's awareness of their lesbian family is a gradual process, for the general public the fact that lesbian women were raising children came as a sudden shock. When it was revealed in 1978 that lesbian women were having babies by donor insemination, headlines such as 'Ban these babies' and 'The most remarkable family in Britain' prompted a huge outcry against lesbian mother families, and calls for laws to stop it.

Child custody disputes

It was also because lesbian women began to fight for custody of their children when they divorced that they became a focus of public attention in the 1970s; but at the time they were fighting a losing battle. Judges almost always granted custody to the heterosexual father rather than to the lesbian mother. This was in direct contrast to what usually happened, as mothers were generally awarded custody in preference to fathers unless they were incapable of adequately caring for their child. If the mother was lesbian, it was considered to be in the child's best interests to remain with the father on the grounds that the mother's sexual orientation would prove harmful to her child. There were two commonly voiced concerns. First, that boys would lose their masculinity and grow up to be homosexual, and that girls would become tomboys and grow up to be lesbian just like their mother. Second, that the children would be teased and bullied at school, lose all their friends and end up psychologically disturbed.[1,2]

At that time no one actually knew what happened to children raised in lesbian mother families, and what the child's best interests really were. Is it better to remain with a lesbian mother to whom they are closely attached? Or to live with a father who provides a heterosexual role model? Judges in child custody cases were commonly faced with questions such as these. The lack of knowledge prompted the first systematic studies of children raised in this way, and it is as a result of this research that we can now begin to answer the question 'Does it make a difference to children whether their parents are heterosexual, lesbian or gay?' The research focused on the concerns raised in custody disputes; the children's gender development as male or female, and their psychological adjustment.

Sissy boys and tomboy girls?

Why is the gender development of children of lesbian parents expected to differ from that of children of heterosexual parents, and what aspects are most likely to be affected? In order to answer these questions we must first look at the various ideas that have been put forward to explain the development of masculinity and femininity in boys and girls.[3] Researchers who study sex differences in behaviour make a distinction between gender identity (whether we think of ourselves as male or female), sex-role behaviour (the behaviours and attitudes associated with being male or female; for example, most boys prefer to play with trucks and trains, and girls with dolls, by the time they are 3 years old), and sexual orientation (whether we are heterosexual, bisexual, lesbian or gay). As we shall see, not all of the theories would predict differences in gender development between children of lesbian and heterosexual mothers. Even those that do would not necessarily expect all aspects – gender identity, sex-role behaviour and sexual orientation – to be affected.

At conception, the father's sperm unites with the mother's egg to form a single cell with twenty-three chromosome pairs. The twenty-third pair is the sex chromosome pair, and determines whether the sex of the child will be male or female. The mother's egg contains an X sex chromosome, and the father's sperm may contain either an X or a Y sex chromosome. If the father's sperm has an X chromosome the child will be female, and if it has a Y chromosome the child will be male. At about six weeks after conception, the embryo develops a gland that produces sex hormones. In a male embryo this gland will produce the male sex hormone testosterone, which causes male internal and external reproductive organs to develop. In a female embryo it is the absence of testosterone that results in the development of female internal and external reproductive organs.

At any point from conception until the baby is born, the development of the embryo may deviate from the normal pattern. There is sometimes an extra X or Y chromosome, or a missing sex chromosome, or the unborn child may be exposed to an overdose, or a deficit, of specific sex hormones. This can happen for two reasons. First, because of an inherited disorder such as congenital adrenal hyperplasia which causes abnormally high levels of testosterone in the embryo, or the androgen insensitivity syndrome which results in abnormally low levels of testosterone. Second, because the mother had been prescribed sex hormones during pregnancy to prevent miscarriage. This practice began in the 1940s and continued into the 1970s, when it became clear not only that this treatment was largely ineffective, but also that women who were prescribed the hormone diethylstilbestrol (DES) were at risk for vaginal and cervical cancer. Studying children and adults who experienced some form of atypical development while still in the womb tells us whether the role of our genes and hormones is only to influence our physical appearance as male or female, or whether it is also to cause differences in behaviour between the sexes.[4]

John Money and his colleagues at Johns Hopkins University examined pseudohermaphrodites (genetic males who are born looking like females and genetic females who are born looking like males). They found that these individuals will identify as either male or female according to the sex in which they are raised.[5] If they are told they are boys, and treated as boys, they will grow up as boys even if they lack a penis, and if they are told they are girls, and treated as girls, they will grow up as girls even if they have a penis instead of a vagina. This led the researchers to conclude that our gender identity largely depends on the sex to which we are assigned at birth, rather than our biology.

However, some doubt has recently been cast on this conclusion from the case of a boy whose penis was accidentally cut off while being circumcised as an infant.[6] The boy was operated on to make him look female, and was raised as a girl. Before puberty, all seemed to be going well. She appeared no different from any other girl. But as adolescence progressed she became more and more unsure of her female identity, and has recently had a sex-change operation to return to being male. On the basis of this example, some researchers have argued that gender identity is biologically based. In addition, in the Dominican Republic, a rare genetic disease that causes children who look and behave like girls to transform into boys at puberty when their male sex hormone levels rise, suggests that biology may play a part in the development of gender identity.[7] But social influences cannot be ruled out as an explanation. The children may simply have responded to the changes in their physical appearance. In fact, they are known about in the Dominican Republic and nicknamed 'guevodoces', meaning 'testicles at 12'. Because fertile men hold a higher status than infertile women (the alternative had they remained female), both the children and the parents would have benefited from the change.

There is less dispute that sex-role behaviour has a biological basis.[4] A preference for guns rather than dolls, or for climbing trees rather than dressing up, seems to be influenced partly by the level of sex hormones circulating in the unborn child, particularly male sex hormones such as testosterone. Girls who have been exposed in the womb to high levels of male hormones, either because they were born with a condition such as congenital adrenal hyperplasia or because their mother had been given hormones during pregnancy to prevent miscarriage, are often tomboys who prefer active play and practical clothes to playing with dolls and pretty dresses. The effects of high levels of female hormones such as progesterone on unborn boys is less clear-cut. Some studies have found them to be less masculine while others have found no difference, possibly because the effects of normal levels of male hormones in boys outweigh the effects of the higher levels of female hormones.

Why is it that some people develop a preference for sexual partners of the other sex, some prefer same-sex partners, and some like both sexes? In recent years there has been an upsurge of interest in biological explanations of sexual orientation. Identical twins of homosexual men,[8] and of lesbian women,[9] have been found to be more likely than non-identical twins to be gay or lesbian themselves. This tells us that sexual orientation may be inherited to some extent. But this does not mean that a homosexual or lesbian sexual orientation is dependent upon a specific genetic pattern. Most genetic effects on behaviour operate indirectly through personality and other characteristics; people with a similar genetic makeup have similar characteristics and, often as a result, similar life experiences.

Another investigation to have attracted a great deal of attention is a study that claims to have identified a genetic marker (a different pattern of genes) on a small section of the X chromosome of some gay men.[10] Of forty pairs of brothers, both of whom were homosexual, thirty-three pairs were found to have the marker. This has led scientists to speculate that there may be a specific gene, yet to be located, that is linked to male homosexuality. But again it does not mean that the presence of this gene, if it exists, determines a homosexual orientation. Neither does it mean that all gay men possess the gene. After all, the marker was not found in seven pairs of brothers. From this study alone, it cannot be concluded that there is a specific gene that 'causes' male homosexuality. We need to know whether the genetic marker is present in heterosexual men, and in lesbian or heterosexual women, before the implications of the finding can be properly understood.

Although the idea that sexual orientation is related to the level of sex hormones in the body after puberty has been popular in the past, studies of sex hormone levels in adults have failed to detect a difference between heterosexual and homosexual men and women. Instead, it is sex hormone levels in the unborn child that may influence sexual orientation in adult life. Women who had been exposed to high levels of testosterone in the womb (those born with congenital adrenal hyperplasia or whose mothers had been given diethylstilbestrol) report greater interest in lesbian relationships than those who had not.[11] However, most of these women are heterosexual, which means that even if prenatal hormones do have some influence on sexual orientation in adulthood, there are other factors that are just as or more important.

There is only one consistent finding that sheds some light on the processes involved in becoming heterosexual or gay; boys who say that they would rather be girls, who dress up in girls' clothes and who prefer dolls and jewellery to cars and trucks, are more likely to prefer partners of the same sex when they grow up.[12] As yet we do not know whether the same is true for girls. Studies have found that lesbian women are more likely than heterosexual women to report tomboyish behaviour when they were young. But whether this difference is real, or simply because lesbian women are more likely than heterosexual women to remember being tomboys, can only be certain when these girls are followed from childhood to find out what happens when they grow up. Just because an association is found between cross-gender behaviour in childhood and a lesbian or gay sexual orientation in adulthood does not mean that this is true of all or even most lesbian women and gay men. Many gay and lesbian adults do not remember these experiences at all, and those men who had been followed up from childhood had originally been seen at a clinic because of their extremely feminine behaviour, so they are not typical of the majority of gay men. Some researchers have suggested that cross-gender behaviour in childhood may result from atypical prenatal hormone levels, but we are far from knowing whether or not this is true. All that can be said for sure is that our sexual orientation is unlikely to be determined by our biology alone.

The first psychologist to examine the processes involved in the development of male and female behaviour was Sigmund Freud, the founder of psychoanalysis. Freud believed that our relationship with our parents early in childhood forms the basis of our personality in adult life.[13] In his lectures and writings early this century, Freud argued that a boy's male identity is dependent upon his successful resolution of the Oedipal conflict at around 5 years of age. The Oedipal conflict is named after the Greek tragedy in which Oedipus unknowingly kills his father and marries his mother. According to Freud, it is at this age that a boy begins to have sexual fantasies about his mother; but although he finds this exciting, it also causes him anxiety. He fears his father's retaliation and, in particular, that if he acts on his sexual urges his father, who is much more powerful, will castrate him. This fear is known as castration anxiety. In order to resolve his conflict between the desire for his mother and the fear of his father, the boy gives up his sexual love for his mother and identifies with his father in the understanding that, because he has a penis, he too will have a female sexual partner when he grows up. In so doing he achieves a secure sense of male sexual identity and power.

Freud believed that girls are also sexually in love with their mother, but he argued that female identity is driven by penis envy rather than castration anxiety.[14] When girls discover that they do not have a penis they believe they have been castrated, and because their mother also lacks a penis they see her as to blame. Girls then turn towards their father as a love object because he has the desired penis. Unlike boys they do not have to give up their love for their father; they do not fear their mother's retaliation because they believe they have already been castrated. Girls' desire for a penis becomes a wish for penetration, and they transfer identification back to their mother and adopt a female role.

According to Freudian theory, boys who fail to identify with their father by the end of the Oedipal period will be less masculine than other boys, and more likely to be gay when they grow up. Girls who do not identify with their mother will be less feminine than other girls, and more likely to become lesbian. But what determines whether boys will identify with their father, and girls with their mother? Children's passage through the Oedipal period is thought to be influenced by the kind of relationship they have with their parents. For boys, the combination of a domineering mother and a weak father is believed to lead to less masculine behaviour in childhood, and a homosexual orientation in adulthood. Less feminine behaviour in girls, and a lesbian sexual orientation, is thought to result from a hostile and fearful relationship with their mother.

Is there any evidence to suggest that this is true? Do gay men have overpowering mothers and submissive fathers, and are the mothers of lesbian women critical and unloving? Although it seemed from early research that the answer was yes, these studies were carried out by psychoanalysts on their patients. Because gay men who opt for psychoanalysis are likely to be different from other gay men – for example, they are more neurotic – and because psychoanalysts' commitment to their theory rules them out as independent researchers, it is difficult to place great weight on these findings. Later studies, not of patients, failed to show a connection between the attitudes and behaviour of parents towards their child and the child's sexual orientation in adult life.

Freud's theory of sexual development caused quite a sensation, and continues to be controversial to this day. A major problem is that it is not possible to test whether children really do have sexual conflicts with their parents. According to Freud, much of sexual development occurs at the unconscious level, and for this reason it is not possible to find evidence to prove the theory right.[3]

Dissatisfaction with the unscientific nature of Freud's explanation of masculinity and femininity led to an exploration of social influences. By the 1970s, through the work of psychologists Albert Bandura and Walter Mischel, it was widely accepted that boys learn to be male and girls learn to be female through their experiences within the family and in their wider social world.[15,16] It was argued that boys and girls are encouraged, through a system of rewards and punishments, to play with toys and take part in activities that are considered to be appropriate for their sex. Thus boys are praised for being strong and brave and playing with guns, and disapproved of for playing with dolls and wearing girlish clothes. Girls are encouraged to play at house, and discouraged from rough-and-tumble games. In this way boys learn to be boys, and girls to be girls. For young children, parents are thought to be key players in bestowing rewards and inflicting punishments. As children grow older, friends, teachers and other adults are considered to play an increasingly important role.

There is a great deal of evidence to show that parents do treat their sons and daughters differently. Right from birth, parents describe their daughters as 'soft' and 'delicate', and their sons as 'alert' and 'strong', even though new-born boys and girls cannot be distinguished on these features. And parents try to ensure that there is no confusion about their children's sex. They dress their daughters in pink and their sons in blue, and give their girls dolls and jewellery and their boys toy trains and trucks.

As infants grow into toddlers, differences in the way that parents treat boys and girls become even more apparent. The psychologist Beverly Fagot went into family homes and observed parents and their children going about their daily lives. She found that girls were given approval for dancing, dressing up in female clothes, playing with dolls, asking for help and following their parents around, and were discouraged from running, jumping, climbing and manipulating objects. Boys, by contrast, were punished for feminine activities, such as playing with dolls and seeking help, and were encouraged to play with toys that were considered to be more appropriate for them, such as building blocks and trucks.[17]

However, just because parents treat their sons and daughters differently does not mean that they are causing their children's masculine and feminine behaviour. Parents may be reacting to differences that would have occurred anyway, rather than creating them. As we have seen, boys and girls appear to some extent to be biologically predisposed to behave according to their sex. The role of parents may simply be to maximise masculine behaviour in their sons and feminine behaviour in their daughters so that small differences in infancy become large differences by the time they reach school age.

Children are also thought to learn to act like boys and girls by modelling their behaviour on people of the same sex as themselves, particularly their mother or father. Thus girls learn to cook and sew because that is what their mothers do, and boys learn to mow the lawn and fix a fuse because that is what their fathers do. But if parents were such important role models for their sons and daughters, we would expect sons to be more like their fathers and daughters to be more like their mothers than is actually the case. And how can we explain boys' liking for cars when it is their mother and not their father who drives the family car? The idea that children directly imitate individuals of the same sex as themselves is now considered to be too simplistic.[18] Instead, it seems that they learn which behaviours are considered appropriate for males and which for females by observing many men and women and boys and girls. They then imitate the behaviours they commonly see to be appropriate for their own sex. So children imitate a wide variety of individuals, of whom parents number only two; and for school-age boys and girls, friends appear to be particularly important as role models. But it is the gender stereotypes that are ever present in our social world, rather than specific people, that seem to be most influential. From infancy, children are bombarded with gender stereotypes of girls being soft and caring and boys being tough. And from as young as 2 years old, not only will they tell you that boys grow up to be doctors and girls nurses, and that boys are brave and girls are weak, but also that they strongly believe that this is true.

Over the past thirty years, the way in which psychologists view children has changed dramatically. Children are no longer thought of as passive creatures at the mercy of their life experiences. Instead, they are seen as active participants in their own development. In becoming masculine or feminine, it seems that boys and girls seek out for themselves information about gender, and socialise themselves as male or female. And as their sense of male or female identity becomes more fixed as they grow older, they become increasingly interested in doing the same as others of their sex. Gender is not simply something that is imposed on children; throughout childhood, they are actively constructing for themselves what it means to be a boy or a girl.[19]

So what does all this tell us? Should we expect the gender identity, sex-role behaviour or sexual orientation of children of lesbian mothers to differ from that of children whose mothers are heterosexual? The answer to this question will depend on which psychologist you ask. Those who favour biological explanations would not expect the experience of growing up in a lesbian family to make any difference to the child, although they may argue for a genetically transmitted effect. Psychoanalytic theorists, on the other hand, stressing the importance of heterosexual parents for the successful resolution of the Oedipal conflict, would expect boys to be less masculine and girls to be less feminine in their identity and behaviour. A lesbian or gay sexual orientation in adulthood may be thought to be particularly likely for boys with a close relationship, and girls with a hostile relationship, with their lesbian mother. Those who subscribe to the view that social influences are paramount would probably reply that it depends on whether lesbian mothers treat their children differently from heterosexual mothers, and on how much their children are exposed to non-traditional stereotypes of male and female roles.

It was in the midst of this lack of certainty about the likely outcomes for children of lesbian mothers that researchers first began to study these families more than twenty years ago. The early investigations conducted in the UK and the USA all compared children of lesbian mothers with children of single heterosexual mothers. The two types of family were alike in that the children were being raised by women in the absence of a father, but differed in the sexual orientation of the mother. Any differences between them could then be assumed to stem from differences in the mother's sexual orientation rather than from the presence or absence of a father in the home.

It was striking how similar the findings of all these studies were, given the different samples studied using different methods in different geographical locations often thousands of miles apart.[20,21,22] The gender identity of children raised by lesbian mothers was found to be in line with their biological sex. These children were not at all confused about their gender identity; the boys were quite sure that they were male, and the girls that they were female. Neither did the sons and daughters of lesbian mothers differ from the sons and daughters of heterosexual mothers in their preference for masculine and feminine toys, games and activities. Given that many lesbian mothers actively encourage their children to be less sex stereotyped in their behaviour, it is interesting that their efforts appear to make no difference at all to the toys and activities chosen by their daughters and sons.

What about sexual orientation? Are children of lesbian mothers more likely than children of heterosexual mothers to be lesbian or gay themselves? From a study of adults who had been raised in lesbian families, the answer seems to be no. Although children of lesbian mothers, particularly daughters, are more likely to consider the possibility of, and experiment with, same-sex relationships, the large majority of both sons and daughters of lesbian mothers identify as heterosexual when they grew up.[23] And, contrary to popular assumption, lesbian mothers did not encourage their children to become lesbian or gay themselves.

'We've talked about her sexuality. She thinks that she is heterosexual. What I want is for her to grow up feeling OK about her sexuality. If she's a lesbian, that's fine. If she's heterosexual, that's fine. No problem.'

'I want her to be happy, and she knows that. And she knows that what is important is the relationship and not the person's gender.'

Teased and bullied?

The other common assumption about the children of lesbian mothers is that they will be teased about their mother's sexual orientation, bullied at school and ostracised by friends. The ability to form lasting friendships is extremely important for children. It is through friendships that they develop social skills and learn how to relate to others. Children who lack this experience become at risk for psychological problems.

Investigations that have focused on friendships have found that before adolescence, children of lesbian mothers are no more likely than children of heterosexual mothers to be teased or bullied by their peers. They are just as popular, and are no more likely to have difficulties in making friends.[20,21] The picture changes during adolescence. They are not teased or bullied more than other children overall, but there is one important difference. Whereas other teenagers are teased about their size or shape or the colour of their skin, children of lesbian mothers are more likely to be teased about their own or their mother's sexuality.[23] This can be upsetting; but whether there will be long-lasting consequences will depend largely or how this is handled at home. Having a lesbian mother who is understanding and supportive goes a long way toward ameliorating any negative effects of being picked on by peers.

For many children, having a lesbian mother does not present a major problem at school:

'I got in the odd scuffle at school about it but it didn't feature in any major way. I got in as many scuffles as any other child about their parents. You know, "My dad's bigger than your dad, or my mum's prettier than your mum." It was that sort of thing. Most of my friends used to love my mother's partner. They'd ring up and she'd be nice to them on the phone and they'd think "Oh, she's nice" and when they came here she was really cool. We would say "Oh we really like this boy at school" and she'd say "Ooh what's he like?" and we'd tell her and she'd say "Ooh you'd better not tell your mother 'cos she won't be very pleased. You're only 12." Even if there was any prejudice it would be gone by the time the children went home because she was such good fun. So it was alright. You know, I think that kids are better at accepting it than adults are. As long as the person is nice to them and they get on.'

But some children from lesbian families are picked on, and rejected by their classmates:

'When I was about 13, my friend found out about my mum. I wasn't allowed to go to her house anymore. Her mum and dad forbade me to go anywhere near. And that hurt me because she had been my best friend for a long, long time. I lost that friend. And then, of course, there was a chain reaction. Everybody found out. They said "Don't go near her, she'll just turn out like her mum, so you don't want to go near her." And I lost a lot of friends through that. But there was one friend who really did stick by me and she's still around today.'

Where a child lives makes a difference. In some neighbourhoods, people are more accepting than in others. And attitudes have also changed over time. This boy, who grew up in an inner city and is now an art student, was aware of a shift in attitude among his friends from the beginning to the end of school:

'School was one big nightmare really, because I got picked on so much. I had cigarettes stubbed out on the back of my neck, and high-heeled shoes thrown at me, and bits of hair cut off, and my head chucked down the loo and that sort of thing. They would say to everyone "Oh, your mum's a lesbian." They were just doing it for a laugh. But by the final year people thought it was really cool. They would say "It's great! Your mum's a lesbian! Wow!" It was almost respected by the end of the year. Everyone thought my mum was cool 'cos she was a lesbian, so it worked out all right.'

Studies of the psychological well-being of children in lesbian families have obtained detailed information from mothers about any behavioural or emotional difficulties shown by their child. This information has then been examined by child psychiatrists to detect psychiatric disorder if it exists. The psychiatrists were not told that the child was from a lesbian family so that their diagnoses would not be biased by such knowledge. Using this procedure in both the UK and the USA, children from lesbian families have been found to be just as well adjusted as children from heterosexual homes.[20,21,22] Teachers' reports have backed up these findings. This is particularly important, as the mothers could have been trying to present their children in the best possible light.

It has sometimes been argued that the psychological damage caused by rearing in a lesbian family will not become apparent until the children grow up. Again, this does not seem to be the case. Young adults who have been raised as children in lesbian mother families are no more likely to be anxious, depressed, or to seek professional help for psychological problems than are young adults raised by heterosexual mothers.[23] So contrary to the concerns that have been expressed about the psychological difficulties that the sons and daughters of lesbian mothers are likely to experience, it seems that they are at no greater risk for emotional or behavioural problems in childhood or adulthood than their peers from heterosexual homes.

Planned lesbian families

A problem with the early research on lesbian families is that the children studied had been born while the mother was still married, and most had lived with their father during their first years of life. To some extent, early family experiences lay the foundations for later psychological development, so what we know about these children cannot necessarily be generalised to children raised by lesbian mothers from the start. But an increasing number of women are becoming parents *after* coming out as lesbian. Some are single mothers; others are couples who have planned their family together and share the parenting role. Pregnancy is achieved in a variety of ways. Some women go to a fertility clinic and are inseminated with the sperm of an anonymous donor; some opt for self-insemination using sperm donated by a male friend, and others have sex with men. Some biological fathers of these children have no contact with the child while others play an important role throughout the child's life.

This woman conceived her child by having sex with a male friend:

> 'I absolutely didn't want to do it by insemination. I wanted to do it by sleeping with a guy. I had a relationship for a few months with a guy I've actually known for years, and we're still friends. He knew I was a lesbian who wanted to get pregnant and he wanted a baby as well.'

But this woman and her partner decided upon donor insemination through a clinic, which meant that they would not know who was the father of their child:

> 'I've always known that I would have a child. But it was getting into this relationship that made it seem feasible. Heterosexual intercourse didn't feel appropriate. Of all the options, going through a clinic was the one I felt most comfortable with. Although there are difficulties around the issue of donor anonymity, at the end of the day I felt I could help my child best with some-thing I felt most comfortable with.'

Sometimes women prefer to know the father and so choose self-insemination:

> 'We thought we would go for a named donor. We thought it would be nice for our child to know there was an identifiable person. We have always told our son who his dad is. He knows he doesn't live with his dad. And he knows he's never been looked after by his dad. But when he could talk he looked at him and said "That's my dad."'

Interestingly, lesbian parents are much more open with their children about the use of donor insemination than are heterosexual parents. In a comparison between lesbian and heterosexual couples who had conceived their child by donor insemination in the Netherlands, it was found that almost all the lesbian mothers had told their children how they had been conceived whereas none of the heterosexual couples had done so.[24]

> 'She knew very early on how I'd conceived her. We explained it to her in quite simple terms and said there are different ways of making a baby and this is one way.'

Studies of this new type of lesbian family are beginning to appear, and tell us about the psychological development of children who grow up in a lesbian family right from birth. From this research, it seems that children who grow up with a lesbian mother from the start are no different from those who make the transition to a lesbian family later in life.[25,26,27,28] One aspect does differ, however. Co-mothers in lesbian families are much more involved in the day-to-day life of their child than are fathers in heterosexual families.

But, in spite of the co-mother's role, she is often not accepted as a parent of the child:

> 'As a non-biological parent you are so invisible. It's just incredible. My partner's family don't accept me as a parent of our daughter. The time we spent with them was horrendous. We stayed with them and they were civil. But it was just the most undermining, humiliating experience. It was quite damaging to all of our relationships. It was the first time our daughter ever came across homophobia in terms of her grandparents not acknowledging me as her parent.'

Gay father families

In recent years attention has turned from lesbian mothers to gay fathers as a source of public outrage. Gay couples who have become fathers with the help of a surrogate mother, and gay couples who have been foster-parents, have been the subject of vitriolic attack. The situation of gay fathers in the 1990s is not unlike that of lesbian mothers in the 1970s.

Many children have fathers who have sex with men, but the majority of these children are unaware of their fathers' gay relationships. Being openly gay generally precludes fathers from having their children live with them. With the odds stacked against them, because they are male as well as gay, most do not even attempt to gain custody of their children if they divorce. As a result, much of the information about children with gay fathers comes from the fathers rather than the children themselves, and many of these fathers have little contact with their children as they grow up.

From the studies carried out so far, it seems that the gender development of the sons and daughters of gay fathers is no different from that of other children.[29] There have been no reports of cross-gender identity of the type associated with a later lesbian or gay sexual orientation, and it appears that sons of gay fathers are just as masculine, and daughters just as feminine, as other boys and girls of their age. Investigations of the sexual orientation of the sons and daughters of gay fathers have suggested that most are heterosexual when they grow up.

Although an in-depth study of the psychological well-being of children of gay fathers has yet to be carried out, the available evidence suggests that the emotional or behavioural problems experienced by children who remain in contact with their gay father after their parents' divorce are more associated with the divorce than with having a gay parent. Estimates vary as to how likely children with gay fathers are to be stigmatised by peers. Whereas many children are concerned about this possibility, it seems that teasing or bullying about the father's sexual identity is rare. This is because children are usually able to discern who can be trusted, and also because gay fathers generally handle this issue sensitively, for example, by not appearing at school with their partner against the child's wishes. Gay fathers often experience considerable anxiety about 'coming out' to their children, and many keep their sexual orientation secret for fear of damaging their relationship with them. In fact, it is unusual for children to reject their father when they find out that he is gay, although they may not necessarily approve of his gay relationships or lifestyle.

In recent years, a small but growing number of gay men have become parents after coming out, often having children with lesbian women and sharing in their upbringing.

'For a very long time I'd wanted to have a child although I didn't think it would be feasible really, being gay. But a close friend of mine who is a lesbian woman wanted to have a child herself so, after lots of discussion about all the issues with her and my partner of thirteen years, we decided to go ahead and try to have a child together. She became pregnant through self-insemination on the second attempt. It was very exciting. Our son lives with his mother and her partner and that is his home. But he spends one or two nights a week with us. He has his own room in our house and considers it home, but not his main home. His grandparents are also very involved in his care. Our neighbours are friendly and supportive but that is probably because we live in a big city. If we were living in a small town I think it would be more difficult. He is very aware that he has two dads and two mums, and I think he understands that this is different from some of his friends who have only got a mum and a dad, or just one mum. He is only 2 years old at the moment and doesn't have much contact with the outside world. But once he goes to school we will have no control over who he meets, or the kinds of comments that the people he is mixing with might make. There will be times when he is made to feel that he comes from some weird, or less good, family because he hasn't got a mummy and a daddy who he lives with. We are going to have to wait for him to be ready to ask us questions and answer them honestly.'

So does it make a difference to children if their mother is lesbian or their father is gay? It seems not. In terms of both gender development and psychological well-being, the two aspects of development that were predicted to be affected, the sons and daughters of lesbian mothers appear to be just the same as any other children. Although less is known about children of gay fathers, the available evidence suggests that they do not differ either. For children who live with gay fathers, the main difficulty they are likely to face is prejudice from the outside world. There is also concern about the potentially harmful effects of the multiple partnerships that are characteristic of the lifestyles of some gay men. However, little is known about the relationships of gay men who are fathers, especially of those who live with their children, or the impact of family life.

This man, who grew up in a lesbian mother family, puts it this way:

> 'I don't think that it has affected me for the worse. I don't think I'm a bad person. I know my failings. But they would have been the same failings if my mum and dad had continued to live together happily ever after.'

Part II

Family relationships

Chapter 5

Quality of relationships between parents and children

Whether children are happy or sad, confident or shy, outgoing or withdrawn, depends, to some extent at least, on the type of relationship they have with their parents. That we know; but if we ask ourselves *how* parents influence their children, and *how much* effect they really have, these questions are much more difficult to answer. If we consider all the different aspects of children's feelings and behaviour that we might be concerned about – whether they feel good about themselves, whether they are well behaved, whether they are popular and whether they are doing well at school – we can see that the answer might be different for each type of behaviour.

Much of the knowledge we have today about what aspects of parenting matter most for children's psychological adjustment comes from the groundbreaking work of the psychiatrist John Bowlby and the psychologist Mary Ainsworth who together taught us about the importance for children of feeling secure in their relationship with their parents. According to John Bowlby, the quality of a child's relationship with his or her mother in the first years of life determines that child's future well-being;[1] children who do not become attached to their mother at this time will be at serious psychological risk as they grow up. His views were most famously encapsulated in a report written for the World Health Organization in 1951[2] in which he stated: 'an infant and young child should experience a warm, intimate, and continuous relationship with his mother (or permanent mother substitute – one person who steadily "mothers" him) in which both find satisfaction and enjoyment.'

Certain of Bowlby's beliefs have now been questioned. It is no longer thought that the mother must be the child's main attachment figure, and it is now generally accepted that children can become attached to more than one person, not least their father. In fact, Bowlby himself changed his views on these issues in his latter years.[3] Children may become attached to one or a few specific individuals, usually in a clear order of preference, and the more a person interacts with an infant the more likely that infant is to become attached to that person. Thus whoever is most involved in looking after the child will become the main attachment figure, and the child will turn to the others when the main attachment figure is not there. More than any other person, John Bowlby has helped us to understand the nature of parent–child relationships, and the ways in which experiences with parents can influence children's psychological development from childhood through to adult life.

Although Bowlby trained as a psychoanalyst and was convinced of the importance of children's relationship with their mother for their future psychological development, he soon came to believe that it would be more informative to study what actually happened to children than what went on in their unconscious minds. His ideas originated from his studies of children who had been separated from their mother. Such children, he found, became very distressed in the short term and, after prolonged separation, showed extremely disturbed behaviour. He was particularly interested in children taken into hospital who, in the 1940s and 1950s when Bowlby was studying them, were allowed little contact with their parents. Bowlby observed that these children all responded in a similar way: at first they made a fuss, and when this failed they gave up in despair; and finally they entered the stage of detachment when they appeared not to care. The longer the spell away from home the more long-lasting were the effects of separation. The heart-rending film made by Bowlby's colleague James Robertson of these children being left by their parents on hospital wards points to just how devastating such separations can be. Further evidence for the negative effects of separating children from their parents came from Bowlby's classic study 'Forty-four juvenile thieves: their characters and home life', which described the inability of some of these young men to form affectionate relationships with anyone, a finding he associated with long periods of separation from their mother early in childhood.[4]

Bowlby was also greatly influenced by the work of ethologists such as Konrad Lorenz who, in his studies of newly hatched goslings, found that these young birds had an innate tendency to follow a moving object, most commonly their mother, and to remain close to her once the attachment had been formed. This behaviour was seen as fulfilling a protective function; those who stayed close were more likely to survive. For Bowlby, these findings were of direct relevance to human behaviour. He argued, in his seminal book *Attachment*,[1] that human infants, like goslings, have an innate tendency to become attached to their mother and, by doing so, also increase their chance of survival. Crying, sucking, looking, smiling and grasping are all behaviours that are present at or soon after birth and have the effect of keeping the mother in close contact with her child. At first, infants cry and smile at anyone but soon they begin to direct their attachment behaviours towards their mother or the person most involved in caring for them. So it is not just what mothers do, but what infants do as well, that leads to the formation of attachment relationships.

Under normal circumstances attachments form when the baby is around 6 to 7 months old. It is at this age that infants begin to be upset when separated from their mother, a phenomenon known as separation anxiety. It is also at this age that they may become distressed in the presence of strangers. According to Bowlby, 6 months to 3 years of age is a 'critical period' for attachment formation; that is, the period when attachments must develop if they are to occur at all. Bowlby's belief in a critical period came from studies of the behaviour of animals, and of human infants, who had been deprived of the opportunity to form attachments in the first year of life. He drew from the ethological studies of Harry Harlow and his colleagues,[5] who found that infant monkeys separated from their mother at birth, and raised in social isolation until they were 6 months old, failed to form normal social relationships in adult life.

Although such experiments could not be carried out on human infants for ethical reasons, children at that time were being kept in orphanages under conditions that were not dissimilar to those experienced by Harlow's monkeys. They were left in cots for most of the day with little human contact, either with adults or other children, and no stimulation of any other kind. Examination of these children showed that although they behaved normally at first, after 6 months of age they became increasingly withdrawn and lost interest in social contact, and by adolescence they had become loners who appeared incapable of forming close attachments to anyone at all. The adverse effects of such an upbringing were found to be particularly marked among those children who had spent their first three years in this way.[6] From these studies, Bowlby concluded that in order for social and emotional development to proceed normally, it is essential that children have the opportunity to form attachments in their first years of life.

More recently it has become evident that attachments can occur after children are 3 years old, although these later attachments may not be so strong. Children adopted into loving homes after spending their first years in an institution can form attachments to their adoptive parents, although it is not unusual for them to be left with social and emotional problems that are difficult to overcome. Recent evidence comes from studies of children raised in the impoverished orphanages of Romania in the 1980s who have shown remarkable recovery from their early experience of social deprivation.[7] It is now thought that the period between 6 months and 3 years of age is the optimal time for attachments to form, but that given the right circumstances children can develop attachments after that time.

Although studies of children denied the opportunity to form attachment relationships have increased our understanding of the importance of attachment for human development, very few children find themselves in this unfortunate situation. Most children do become attached to their parents or caregivers, but not all become securely attached to them. Mary Ainsworth was particularly interested in the ways in which securely and insecurely attached children differ from each other, and devised the Strange Situation Test as a means of exploring these differences.[8]

The Strange Situation Test involves a series of three-minute episodes in which the mother and infant are observed in an unfamiliar playroom. A number of increasingly distressing events occur, each designed to elicit attachment-related behaviour in the infant. These include the ability to use the mother as a safe haven from which to explore the new surroundings, separation from the mother when the mother is asked to leave the room, and being left alone with a stranger. The infant is closely observed and particular attention is paid to his or her exploration of the playroom when the mother is present, response to the stranger, reaction to the mother leaving the room and, in particular, behaviour towards the mother on her return. The way in which babies reunite with their mother after a period of separation is viewed as an indicator of how much they expect to receive comfort from her when they are distressed.

Ainsworth identified three patterns of behaviour shown by infants in the Strange Situation Test. Some were confident about exploring the room and playing with the toys in their mother's presence, were not distressed by the arrival of the stranger when their mother was there, greeted their mother warmly on her return from leaving the room and, if they had been upset by her absence, were easily comforted by her and soon returned to play. Such infants were considered to be securely attached.

Infants who were designated as insecurely attached behaved in one of two ways. Those classified as 'insecure-resistant' often seemed wary of exploring the playroom even when their mother was present, became extremely distressed when their mother left the room, and on her return clearly wanted to turn to her but resisted contact and were difficult to comfort. In contrast, 'insecure-avoidant' infants tended to explore the playroom immediately, showed little distress when the mother left the room, and little interest in her return. Instead, they would often carry on with whatever they were doing and appear to ignore her presence. More recently a fourth category, 'insecure-disorganised', has been identified. Unlike the insecure-resistant children who are distressed by the Strange Situation Test, and the insecure-avoidant children who show a lack of concern, these children do not seem to have a consistent way of responding to stress. Instead they appear disoriented by the experience, sometimes becoming completely motionless as if frozen to the spot, or moving in odd ways in their mother's presence.[9] This pattern of behaviour is most often seen among children who have been neglected or abused and is thought to result from frightening (in the case of mothers who have inflicted trauma on the child) or frightened (in the case of mothers who have experienced trauma) behaviour by the mother.

Although it is widely accepted that infants' responses to the Strange Situation Test reflect their security of attachment, some critics have suggested that what is really being measured is the infant's temperament.[10] Right from birth some babies cry a lot and are difficult to soothe whereas others are relatively calm and easy to handle. What the Strange Situation Test is measuring, it is argued, is not the baby's security of attachment but the baby's temperament, particularly the baby's vulnerability to stress. Irritable infants, for example, may be more likely to cry and be difficult to settle after separation from their mother, and therefore more likely to be classified as insecurely attached. Attachment theorists dispute this alternative explanation on the grounds that many infants obtain different attachment classifications with different attachment figures; that is, their behaviour in the Strange Situation Test is specific to the particular relationship being examined. If their response to the Strange Situation Test was due to the infant's temperament rather than security of attachment to a specific person, it would be expected that their attachment classification would be the same regardless of which attachment figure took part.

In a recent analysis of fourteen different investigations of infants' attachment to their mother and their father separately, involving almost a thousand families, it was shown that 62 per cent of infants did obtain the same classification with both parents.[11] Of the 38 per cent who did not, 48 per cent were securely attached to their mother and insecurely attached to their father, and 52 per cent were securely attached to their father and insecurely attached to their mother. The finding that some infants do have the same attachment classification with each parent and some do not leaves the matter unresolved with those who favour the temperament explanation emphasising the concordance, and attachment theorists emphasising the lack of concordance, between babies' attachment to their mother and their father. The answer most probably lies between the two positions, with the patterns of behaviour shown by infants in the Strange Situation Test reflecting an interaction between temperament and security of attachment. After all, it is easier for mothers to have a positive relationship with a calm and sociable baby than with an irritable one which, in turn, increases the likelihood that the former baby will become securely attached.

Most studies have focused on children's attachment to their mother rather than their father. This is partly because children's main attachment figure is usually the mother and also because mothers are generally more involved than fathers in the day-to-day care of their children and so are easier to engage in research. But as we have seen in Chapter 2, children do form attachments to their father and from the findings of the fourteen studies reported above where children's attachment to both parents was assessed, the proportion of children securely attached to their father was almost identical to the proportion classified as securely attached to their mother.

We know that children who lack the opportunity to form attachments at all are likely to experience psychological problems in later life, but what about children who are insecurely attached? Are these children also at risk? A number of studies have addressed this question by using the Strange Situation Test to classify children as securely or insecurely attached and then following them up to determine whether the insecurely attached children are disadvantaged in comparison with their securely attached counterparts with respect to various aspects of social and emotional development.

Many studies have identified a link between attachment security in infancy and various aspects of behaviour in later childhood.[12,13,14,15,16] Securely attached children are, for example, more likely to play enthusiastically and co-operatively, have high self-esteem, be popular with other children, interact positively with visitors to their home, show independence at school, show competence in carrying out problem-solving tasks and ask for help when appropriate. It seems, therefore, that secure attachment relationships in infancy are associated with more positive outcomes for children in the pre-school and early school years. But it is not inevitable that children who have insecure attachments in the first years of life will have difficulties as they grow up; nor do all securely attached infants grow into well-adjusted children. In order to fully understand the development of attachment relationships we must be aware not only of the role of the child's temperament but also of the wider social context in which these relationships are formed.

The importance of the social circumstances in which mothers and their babies live is highlighted by an investigation of the relationship between attachment security in infancy and the development of psychological disorder at the time of entering school. Children took part in the Strange Situation Test at age 1 and were then assessed for the presence of behaviour problems when they were 6 years old.[17] It was found that boys who were insecurely attached to their mother in infancy were more likely to show behaviour problems at 6 years old, with 40 per cent of insecurely attached boys showing later behaviour problems. There was no such relationship for girls. It seemed, therefore, that there was a connection between early insecurity and the later development of behaviour problems for boys, but it is important to remember that 60 per cent of the insecure boys did not show problems at age 6. In seeking to establish what differentiated the insecure boys who developed problems from the insecure boys who did not, the researchers found that it was the combination of insecure attachment and exposure to stress such as their family's social isolation that was most likely to result in behaviour problems for the child.

Similarly, in an investigation of irritable babies and their mothers, it was found that infants whose mothers had little social support from family and friends were more likely to become insecurely attached than those whose mothers had high levels of social support and were thus in a better position to cope with the demands of a difficult baby.[18] Once again it seems that the type of attachment an infant will form depends, at least in part, on outside pressures on family life. As the following chapters will show, there are many different influences on children's lives that shape the course of their development as they grow up. Secure attachment in infancy provides children with strong roots from which to grow but does not determine whether they will flourish.

To the extent that secure attachment provides children with a good start in life it is important to know what makes a securely attached child, and why it is that some children form insecure attachments. Mary Ainsworth was not simply interested in the characteristics of securely and insecurely attached infants but also turned her attention to addressing this question. She observed large numbers of mothers and their babies over long periods of time, both in Africa and the United States, and found a link between the mother's behaviour towards her infant and the type of attachment the infant had to the mother.[19,20] Mothers of securely attached infants tended to be responsive to their infants and sensitive to their needs. They were also affectionate; they smiled, talked to and touched their infants a great deal, and engaged in what Bowlby termed 'synchronised routines' with them. Synchronised routines are like conversations without words, exchanges which involve both the mother and the baby and which both enjoy. First the infant may look at the mother, the mother may respond by saying something back, then the infant smiles, the mother smiles back, and so on. According to Bowlby and Ainsworth, the better mothers and infants are at building up synchronised routines, the more likely it is that the infant will become securely attached.

Mothers of insecure-resistant infants appear to be unpredictable in their behaviour. Sometimes they are responsive to their infants but at other times they are unavailable or unresponsive to them, and sometimes they misinterpret their infant's signals, respond inappropriately and have difficulty in establishing synchro-nised routines. The ambivalent nature of the infant's response to the mother on reunion with her in the Strange Situation Test, seeking contact but resisting it, is thought to reflect the infant's uncertainty about whether she will be comforting. In contrast, mothers of insecure-avoidant infants appear to be actively rejecting. They are often unresponsive to their infant's signals, don't cuddle them much and can be impatient with them. In the Strange Situation Test it seems that these infants have learned to defend themselves against rejection by showing little emotion and avoiding their mother on her return. Mothers of insecure-resistant infants and of insecure-avoidant infants have been respectively described as unpredictably responsive and predictably unresponsive in comparison with the predictably responsive behaviour of mothers of securely attached infants.[21]

Over the years there has been some controversy about the origins of secure and insecure attachment relationships, not only about the importance of mothers responding sensitively to their infants but also about the aspects of maternal sensitivity that make a difference. Whether maternal sensitivity in its narrow sense of recognising and responding promptly and appropriately to the infant's signals is the key to secure attachment rather than other maternal behaviours, such as affection and close physical contact, are questions that have interested researchers for some time, culminating in 1997 in a review of all studies to have investigated whether a mother's sensitivity is associated with the attachment security of her baby.[22] From a statistical analysis of all of the studies combined, it was concluded that maternal sensitivity is an important factor in whether or not infants will become securely attached; infants whose mothers respond appropriately and promptly to their signals are almost twice as likely to become securely attached. However, this does not mean that all infants with sensitive mothers become securely attached or that all infants whose mothers do not respond sensitively develop an insecure attachment relationship. Other aspects of parenting, it seems, are also at play in the formation of early attachment relationships including the mother's expression of affection and the amount of stimulation she gives to her baby. Maternal sensitivity goes some way towards explaining why some infants develop secure, and others insecure, attachments to their mother, but it is not the whole answer. Much remains to be understood about the origins of secure and insecure attachments not least the contribution of the child itself, an issue that will be considered in Chapter 7.

We are also left with the question of why some mothers are more sensitive than others. Are some mothers simply better at understanding and responding to their infants' needs? Or does her sensitivity depend on what other demands there are on her attention? It would seem likely that mothers who are raising their children under difficult conditions may have less opportunity to respond sensitively to their infant's every need. As we shall see in the following chapters, mothers who have a hostile relationship with their husband or partner, or who are struggling to make ends meet, are likely to have difficulty in giving their full attention to their child. Whereas the infant's crying may cause her to pick up and soothe her baby when she is feeling calm, her inclination when she is under stress may be quite the reverse.

Central to Bowlby's theory is the concept of 'internal working models' of attachment relationships, the idea that through our early experiences with our mother, or other attachment figures, we build up pictures of these relationships in our mind.[1] According to Bowlby, these internal working models influence not only our expectations of, and behaviour towards, our attachment figures but also how we come to see ourselves. Thus securely attached children would have an internal working model of their mother as available and responsive, and an internal working model of themselves as lovable. Insecure-resistant children would have an internal working model of their mother as someone they could not depend on to be available when they needed her whereas insecure-avoidant children would have an internal working model of their mother as someone they would not expect to be available when they needed her. Both types of insecure children, argued Bowlby, would be likely to have an internal working model of himself or herself as someone who is unworthy of being loved. Our internal representations of attachment figures, and of the self, are believed to influence our relationships with others as we grow up through childhood and into adult life.

Much of the early research on attachment focused on the first two years of life and used the Strange Situation Test to observe infants' behaviour. Although observing actual behaviour proved fruitful in studying attachment in infancy, this approach is less appropriate for examining the attachment relationships of older children. The older children become, what is going on in their unconscious minds cannot necessarily be assessed by simply observing their behaviour. The growing interest in internal working models has presented new challenges in terms of the measurement of attachment, and new techniques have been developed that focus on thought and language as a way of tapping into internal representations of attachment relationships.[23] For example, children might be shown pictures of a child being separated from his or her parents and asked to talk about how they think the child in the picture would feel, or they might be asked to give the ending to a story involving a child in distress. These procedures have been shown to be good indicators of how children view their relationships with their attachment figures.

A question that has been of particular interest to researchers of attachment in recent years is the extent to which the type of attachment the infant forms with the mother or primary attachment figure remains stable over time. Put more simply, 'Is an insecurely attached infant destined to become an insecurely attached child?' One way to answer this question is to establish whether attachment security is related to later development in meaningful ways; that is, whether secure attachment leads to well-adjusted children. As already discussed, studies that have followed up securely and insecurely attached children to examine various aspects of their social and emotional development later in childhood have found some evidence to support the expectation that securely attached infants would do better than their insecurely attached counterparts. But as we saw, secure attachment in infancy did not guarantee well-adjusted children; children's psychological development was also affected by their family circumstances as they grew up.

A more direct approach is to assess children in the Strange Situation Test on more than one occasion to examine whether their classification remains the same over time. These studies have shown that secure infants can become insecure, and that insecure infants can become secure, depending on whether the circumstances of their lives have changed for better or worse. Previously secure children, for example, can become insecure if their family is placed under stress, perhaps if a parent has become unemployed or seriously ill.

The growing interest in the assessment of attachment in later childhood has given researchers the opportunity to examine whether attachment classifications in infancy remain the same in the early school years. Studies in the United States[24] and in Europe[25] have assessed children's attachment security at a year old using the Strange Situation Test, and again at age 6 using a modification of the Strange Situation Test that focuses on the child's behaviour towards the mother on reunion following a one-hour separation. Although the behaviours of interest in the Strange Situation Test when used with infants, such as crying or intense physical contact, are not relevant for 6-year-olds, other aspects of their behaviour, including how they greet their mother on her return and whether they talk freely to her about what has been happening in her absence, are considered to be good indicators of quality of attachment. A child who seems pleased by the mother's return, gravitates towards her and tells her what he or she has been doing in the past hour would be classified as securely attached. An insecure-resistant child might show a mixture of intimacy and hostility, and an insecure-avoidant child would give the mother a cool greeting or even ignore her, keeping quite distant, and would be unlikely to strike up a conversation. When children have been given an attachment classification first at age 1 and again at age 6 by researchers who were not told of their attachment status at age 1, the large majority were found to have the same type of attachment on both occasions. This suggests that although attachment relationships can change, in most cases the type of attachment formed with the mother during infancy remains stable throughout the pre-school years.

The idea that the type of attachment formed in infancy will remain stable as the child grows up, so that insecure infants will become insecure children and insecure adults, is an important tenet of attachment theory. Although the finding that some children can change their attachment classification suggests that attachment theorists are wrong to emphasise the importance of early attachment relationships for later development, Bowlby believed that an infant's attachment classification could change in the early years if there was a change in the infant's relationship with the attachment figure.

A major breakthrough in attachment research in recent years has been the development of the Adult Attachment Interview by Mary Main.[26] This interview, designed to assess adults' internal working models of their attachment relationships, has provided a means not only of studying attachment in adulthood but also of examining links between parents' attachment relationships and those of their children. During the interview, which must be conducted by highly trained researchers, information is obtained about the person's childhood experiences with attachment figures and how these experiences are currently viewed. The material of interest is not so much the actual content of the accounts but how individuals talk about their experiences. In discussing issues such as whether they had ever felt rejected in childhood, the coherence of their accounts, the ease with which they remember and can talk about past events and how they now understand the past have proved to be more informative to researchers than their actual experiences.

On the basis of a person's response to the interview, he or she is classified according to one of four patterns of attachment. People classified as 'autonomous-secure' can talk easily about their relationship with their parents. They give coherent and consistent accounts of their childhood experiences with them and are open about both positive and negative aspects of the relationship. A secure childhood is not necessary for people to be given this classification but if their childhood was difficult they must have come to an understanding of how that came about. The 'dismissing-detached' classification includes people who dismiss attachment relationships as having little importance in their lives. They often describe their parents positively but can provide little supportive evidence, and may even describe events that contradict their statements about a happy family life. They tend not to remember much about their relationship with their parents, although they can remember other aspects of their childhood, and express little concern about unhappy experiences in the past. Those given the classification 'preoccupied-entangled' still appear to be involved in unresolved struggles with their parents and trying to please them, and often appear confused or angry with them. It seems difficult for them to break free, and they often describe conflicts with their parents that are still ongoing. The fourth classification, 'unresolved-disorganised', applies to people who have experienced the traumatic loss of, or separation from, an attachment figure, or neglect or abuse, and who are still preoccupied with unresolved issues from the past.

One of the most interesting findings to emerge from research using the Adult Attachment Interview is that the quality of a woman's childhood relationship with her mother appears to be related to the quality of that woman's relationship with her own child. This suggests that the type of attachment a daughter has with her mother can be passed on from one generation to the next. Evidence for this phenomenon comes from studies that have assessed both the mother's attachment classification and that of her child.[27] These studies have consistently shown that autonomous-secure mothers most often have securely attached children and that mothers with an insecure Adult Attachment Interview classification are most likely to have an insecurely attached child. There is also some evidence that the different classifications of the Adult Attachment Interview are associated with the different types of insecure attachment in childhood. Dismissing-detached mothers tend to have avoidant children, and the children of unresolved-disorganised mothers are most likely to be classified as insecure-disorganised themselves. Although some researchers have also found a tendency for preoccupied-entangled mothers to have insecure-resistant children the evidence for this connection is weak. Of particular interest is a study that found a link between the mother's attachment classification and that of her infant when the mother's interview was conducted before the child was born and thus could not have been influenced by her actual relationship with her child.[28] In this study it was possible to successfully predict in 75 per cent of cases whether the infant would be securely or insecurely attached on the basis of the mother's attachment classification made during pregnancy. By chance alone this would have been true of only 50 per cent.

The suggestion that patterns of attachment may be transmitted from one generation to the next has led to speculation about the ways in which this might happen.[21,27,29] One idea is that parents' internal working models of their attachment relationships may influence their behaviour towards the child, in particular their ability to respond sensitively to their child, which in turn will influence the child's security of attachment. Thus it has been suggested that autonomous parents who have a positive view of their childhood attachment relationships, or have come to terms with their unhappy experiences, may be better able to respond to their infant's needs than dismissing or preoccupied parents; dismissing parents might rebuff children's attachment behaviour in stressful situations because behaviours such as crying may trigger unwanted attachment-related memories in themselves, and preoccupied parents may still be focused on their own attachment experiences and therefore unable to fully attend to their infant. But the mechanism linking mothers' classification on the Adult Attachment Interview to their infants' classification on the Strange Situation Test is far from understood. The mother's attachment status does not have a one-to-one relationship with her responsiveness to her baby and, as we have already seen, maternal responsiveness does not fully explain the type of attachment the baby has to her. Other factors must also be at work.

Another explanation, which is purely speculative at present, is that the connection which exists between an adult's attachment classification and that of the child results from a tendency for the temperamental characteristics of parents to be genetically transmitted to their children. Thus autonomous-secure adults may be more likely to have secure children not because of the way in which they behave towards them but because children have inherited the same characteristics as their parents. Even so, the fact that some children of autonomous parents are insecurely attached, and vice versa, tells us that the attachment classification of parents does not necessarily determine the type of attachment shown by their child.

Does the connection between a mother's attachment classification and that of her child mean that the course of our psychological development may be fixed in childhood, and that what happens to us later in life will make little difference to how we turn out? It seems not. Bowlby believed that the type of attachments we form become more resistant to change beyond the pre-school years but that change can take place. The experience of secure relationships with others in adolescence and adulthood can make up for less satisfactory relationships with parents, as can therapy, both of which can cause us to re-evaluate and come to terms with unhappy relationships in our past.

But not everyone in the field is convinced that security of attachment in adulthood is directly related to childhood attachment security. Instead, the Adult Attachment Interview may simply be measuring a person's current view of attachment relationships and may be unrelated to his or her security of attachment in infancy.[29] In order to address this question it would be necessary to follow up individuals over many years, obtaining their Strange Situation Test classification in infancy and their Adult Attachment Interview classification when they grow up. The few studies that have been conducted so far have failed to find a direct link between a person's security of attachment as a baby and as an adult. However, if account is taken of positive and negative experiences in that person's family life it seems that changes in attachment can be explained in a meaningful way. Insecure babies are more likely to become secure adults if their attachment relationships change for the better, and secure babies are more likely to become insecure adults if their attachment relationships change for the worse. Although we do not yet have an answer to the question of how likely it is that our attachments will remain the same as we grow up, it does seem that our security or insecurity is not fixed for life in infancy but is open to change, depending on other experiences in our lives.

In general, it seems that securely attached children fare better than their insecurely attached counterparts; whether or not a child is securely attached has been shown to have implications for many aspects of his or her psychological development including self-esteem, popularity with peers, and emotional well-being at home and at school. But not all insecurely attached children do badly; neither is it guaranteed that securely attached children will do well. What this research shows us is that secure attachment is *more likely* to result in positive outcomes for the child.[30] Other factors also contribute including aspects of the child's family situation, the child's wider social environment and the child's own personality. The quality of parent–child relationships does matter, but not completely, and not in isolation. In Chapter 6 we shall look at the impact of the parents' relationship with each other, and of their own psychological well-being, from the perspective of the child. Attachment is not the only important element in the relationship between parents and their children. Other aspects of parenting, such as the ability to control and discipline their children appropriately, are also essential and will be discussed in Chapter 6.

Chapter 6

Quality of marriage and parents' psychological state

Common sense tells us that living with parents who seem not to like each other, who may be constantly bickering or not talking to each other, or who often fight, is not pleasant for children. But what exactly are the consequences of an unhappy marriage for children? And just how bad does it have to be before they are affected?

The research of John Gottman shows that marriages can go wrong in different ways.[1,2] What troubled marriages have in common is that couples are more likely to criticise, blame and be angry with each other than to show affection, agree and give approval. They are also more likely to respond to anger and criticism from their partner by directing even greater anger and criticism back towards them. In this way fighting can escalate, and may sometimes end in violence.

Much of the evidence that unhappy marriages are bad for children comes from the clinical work of child psychologists and psychiatrists who frequently see the results of troubled marriages in their consulting rooms. It is not unusual for their young patients to come from homes where the relationship between their parents is one of discord and hostility rather than love and affection, and the connection between problems in the marriage and the psychological problems of children is not hard to see.

Surprisingly, however, when systematic studies were carried out of the association between bad marriages and negative outcomes for children, the link between the two was not as strong as expected. Why should this be? Did it really not matter to children how their parents got on, or was there another explanation for these findings? A closer look showed that many of the studies examined how the parents themselves felt about their marriage; that is, whether or not they were satisfied with their relationship with their partner. Marital dissatisfaction in itself had little effect on children; what did make a difference to children was marital conflict. It was those children who saw their parents fight who were most at risk for difficulties themselves.[3,4]

Children whose parents are in conflict are more likely to show conduct problems than emotional disorders.[5,6] They are more aggressive, disobedient and difficult to control than children whose parents are happily married. They are also more likely to become involved in delinquent behaviour, perform poorly at school, and be disliked by peers. Of particular concern is the recent finding that young people with conduct problems are more likely to be violent to their partners when they grow up.[7] As marital conflict is associated with conduct disorders in children it seems that aggressive behaviour towards one's partner is being passed on from one generation to the next. Emotional problems such as anxiety and depression, although less common, can also occur in response to hostility between parents.

But just because parents fight does not mean that their children will suffer psychological problems. Almost all children see their parents argue and most are not affected. In fact, it is thought that it can be good for children to be exposed to arguments because they learn how to resolve disagreements and how to make up. Even children whose parents fight a lot will not necessarily be at risk. After all, some very happily married couples always seem to be arguing. What seems to matter for children is not whether their parents fight but how they fight.[4,5]

So what aspects of conflict between parents are harmful to children? In general, the frequency of arguments does seem to make a difference; the more often parents fight, the worse it is for children. It has sometimes been suggested that children get used to fighting; if their parents often fight they will not notice or become upset. In fact, the opposite is true. It seems that the more parents fight, the more sensitised children become, and the greater the impact on how they feel.

But it seems that children also take account of the context in which the fighting occurs. Does each row signal one further step towards their parents' separation? Or do the children believe that their parents really love each other in spite of their bad feeling? Research has shown that the first situation is more likely to be upsetting for children. Just how hostile parents are towards each other also makes a difference, as does the way in which they fight. Physical violence is much more damaging than arguing, although children are also sensitive to hostility between parents even when they don't actually argue. Simply not speaking to each other, or not looking each other in the eye, is enough to alert children to the fact that their mother and father are not getting on. Physical violence between parents also increases the risk of physical abuse to the child. Taking account of all the available research, Terrie Moffitt and Avshalom Caspi have recently estimated that the risk of child abuse is between three and nine times greater in homes where adult partners hit each other.[7]

It is particularly upsetting for children to be the subject of their parents' rows. In a study of 11- and 12-year-olds by John Grych and Frank Fincham, children were asked to listen to tapes of disagreements between adults and to imagine that the adults were their parents.[8] They were then asked to rate how they felt. Some of the disagreements were related to the child, for example, about childrearing issues such as who should take the child out at the weekend, and other disagreements were unrelated to the child. The researchers found that the children felt more to blame for the disagreement, more ashamed, and more afraid that they themselves would become involved when the conflict concerned them.

Another important factor in how children respond to fighting between their parents is how the parents resolve the conflict.[9] If they do not see their parents make up, or if the parents do not seem genuinely sorry, or fail to reach a compromise that both are happy with, children are more likely to remain angry and upset.

The way in which marital conflict affects children has been the subject of much debate. One group of researchers has argued that marital conflict is bad for children because of its indirect effects on parenting; parents who are in conflict find it difficult to give sufficient attention to their children.[10] Another group has suggested that exposure to parents' fighting has a direct effect on children's psychological well-being; that is, seeing their parents argue is, in itself, distressing.[5,6]

Those who favour the explanation that marital conflict disrupts parenting suggest that parents who are wrapped up in their own disputes will not properly monitor or discipline their children. Diane Baumrind has identified four styles of parenting, each of which she associates with particular outcomes for children.[11] Authoritarian parents are very controlling, expect their children to do as they say, and rarely negotiate with them. Their children are more likely than other children to be defiant, socially incompetent and dependent. Permissive parents are loving parents but exert little control over their children's behaviour and make few demands of them. As a result the children tend to be aimless, lacking in self-assertiveness and uninterested in achievement. Rejecting-neglecting parents either reject or neglect their children. They are not supportive and do not monitor what their children are doing. The children of these parents tend to be the most likely to develop emotional problems and to perform poorly at school. The most positive style of parenting according to Baumrind is an authoritative style, combining warmth and affection with firm control. Authoritative parents control their children's behaviour through negotiation rather than through punishment and exertion of power. These children are more likely to be self-controlled, responsible, co-operative and self-reliant than children of the other types of parents.

The work of Gerald Patterson has also increased our understanding of effective and ineffective ways of controlling children's behaviour.[12,13] His research has shown that when parents react to their children's antisocial behaviour in either an accepting or positive fashion, the children will be more likely to behave badly in future in order to get their own way. Parents who, for example, give in to their child's demands for a new toy in order to prevent a tantrum in the toy store, will find that their child behaves even more unpleasantly the next time around. This pattern of coercive behaviour is particularly common among families with a child who has a conduct disorder.

When parents are in conflict, it is argued, they may be less effective at controlling their children's behaviour, either by becoming inconsistent in their approach to discipline or by becoming less likely to adopt an authoritative approach. Evidence that this may be the case comes from a study that assessed marital conflict and both inconsistency in enforcing discipline and discipline strategies such as authoritarian control and disciplining without punishment. Although mothers and fathers responded differently for sons and daughters, the findings showed poorer discipline of children among parents who were not getting on.[14]

Another way in which marital conflict may disrupt parenting is by interfering with parents' emotional relationships with their children. As discussed in Chapter 5, parents who are emotionally available to their children, are sensitive to their needs and respond appropriately to them are most likely to have securely attached children. Hostility between parents, it has been suggested, may result in more negative relationships with children, either in the form of hostility towards the children or lack of involvement with them, and thus jeopardise the security of children's attachment to their parents. One study which showed just that involved the assessment of the quality of the parents' relationship before the child was born and the child's security of attachment when aged between 1 and 3 years old. A high level of conflict between parents before the birth was found to be associated with the child's insecure attachment 3 to 5 years later.[15]

Some studies have indicated that marital conflict has a more deleterious effect on fathering than mothering. Why this should be so is not absolutely clear, although one idea is that because fathers are less involved than mothers in day-to-day parenting it is easier for them to withdraw from their children when difficulties arise in their marriage. In a recent review of all investigations to have assessed the parenting of both mothers and fathers in the same family, it was concluded that although fathering is more adversely affected by marital conflict than mothering, the quality of parenting of both mothers and fathers deteriorates when they are in dispute.[16]

Evidence that hostility between parents, in itself, has negative consequences for children's psychological well-being comes from a series of experiments by E. Mark Cummings and his colleagues.[5] In these experiments, children were exposed to arguments between adults and their reactions monitored. What the researchers consistently found was that simply being exposed to adults' arguments, even if the arguments did not involve them, was distressing for children. Some cried or looked upset, some were frightened and some became angry and aggressive themselves. Not only did they look agitated and upset, they showed physical signs of distress as well, such as increased blood pressure and heart rate. Children of all ages have been studied with similar results, and even babies as young as 6 months old were found to become distressed.

So it seems that marital conflict may have indirect and direct effects on the psychological well-being of children; as well as interfering with the relationship between the parents and the child, hostility between parents appears to be upsetting in its own right. Evidence that both processes are at work comes from a recent study of 370 young adolescents followed up over a period of two years.[17] An indirect effect of marital conflict on the relationship between parents and children was found; parents who were more hostile to each other were also more hostile to their child. There was also a direct relationship between the frequency of marital conflict and the level of the child's psychological distress.

In trying to understand marital conflict from the point of view of the child, it has been suggested that it is the meaning of the conflict that determines its psychological impact.[4] A fight between parents who are always arguing would be expected to produce more distress than a fight between parents who generally get on well. Similarly, an argument that involves the child, perhaps about which parent should stay at home to baby-sit while the other goes out, would also be expected to be more distressing. As already discussed, there is some evidence from the study by John Grych and Frank Fincham[8] that children do feel more upset by disagreements that involve them. This same study also demonstrated that the more intense the conflict, the worse children felt. It seems, therefore, that the child's interpretation of the conflict will determine the impact of the conflict on the child.

An alternative, but complementary explanation for differences in children's reaction to hostility between their parents places greater emphasis on the implications of marital conflict for their emotional security.[9] It is argued that children's emotional security is dependent not just on the quality of their relationship with their parents but also on the quality of their parent's relationship with each other, and whether or not children will develop psychological problems as a result of conflict between their parents will depend on the implications of the conflict for their emotional security. Put another way, the more children experience hostility between their parents, the greater the threat to their emotional security, and the greater the risk that they will develop behavioural and emotional problems.

As a way of assessing the extent to which children tend to view fighting between their parents as a threat to their emotional security, Patrick Davies and E. Mark Cummings asked 6- to 9-year-old children to listen to a tape-recording of a man and woman fighting, and to imagine that the argument was taking place between their parents.[18] The children were then asked how they thought the scene would end in their own home. Those children whose parents had the most hostile marriages were most likely to see the argument ending in a way that was threatening to their own well-being and to family life. For example, they were more likely to say that the fight would get worse with the parents shouting and swearing, and that in the long term they might split up or divorce. More importantly, children who felt that their own security was at risk because of the quarrelling between parents were more likely to show psychological problems, particularly anxiety.

Almost without exception, investigations of the impact of the quality of parents' marriage on the development of children have focused on the adverse effects of hostile marriages rather than on the beneficial effects of harmonious marriages. It seems likely that the more favourable outcomes for children of happily married parents do not simply result from the absence of serious conflict but instead are more directly associated with positive aspects of the relationship such as the way in which the couple communicate with each other and show each other affection. This area of research is currently in its infancy, but it has the potential to increase our understanding of which types of marriage are good for children and not just which are bad.

Another part of the equation that has largely been neglected in the link between marital conflict and children's psychological problems is the role played by the child. It is almost always assumed that hostility between parents causes problems in the child. But it is conceivable, in some families at least, that it is the child who triggers the conflict between the parents. A boy with conduct problems, who is aggressive or disobedient, not only produces stress in the family, in itself likely to increase parents' quarrelling, but may also cause the parents to disagree about how to discipline his difficult behaviour.

Large-scale longitudinal studies that have demonstrated an increase in children's behaviour problems in the years leading up to their parents' divorce have tended to explain this phenomenon as the result of conflict in the marriage prior to the divorce.[19] An alternative explanation is that parents of difficult children are more likely to divorce because of the pressure that such children place on the marriage. Although the research evidence considered in this chapter shows that marital conflict can cause psychological problems in children, the alternative explanation should not be ruled out. It is entirely conceivable that children themselves can contribute to conflict between their parents, and in so doing not only cause their parents to be hostile to each other but also to them. Although research is lacking on the ways in which children may cause conflict between their parents, the more general influences of children's own behaviour on family functioning will be discussed in more detail in Chapter 7.

It is not just the quality of their parents' marriage, but also their parents' psychological adjustment that can impact upon the psychological well-being of children. Living with a mother or father who has a psychiatric disorder can take its toll. Among the many studies of the consequences for children of their parents' psychiatric disorder, parental depression has received the greatest attention. Children of depressed parents have consistently been found to show elevated rates of behavioural, social and emotional problems. Of particular interest are the findings of studies that have made a diagnosis of the presence or absence of psychiatric disorder in both children and their parents. These findings tell us that children whose parents are depressed are not only more likely to show a wide range of psychological problems but are also more likely to become depressed themselves.

In a study of 200 families, Myrna Weissman found that children of depressed parents were three times more likely to be diagnosed as having a psychiatric disorder than children whose parents were not depressed, and the risk was even greater when both parents had psychiatric problems.[18] The most common diagnosis among the children of depressed parents was depression. Thirteen per cent were diagnosed with depression compared with none of the comparison group, 5 per cent had wished they were dead and 1 per cent had made a suicide attempt. These figures were based on information obtained from the children's parents. When the children themselves were interviewed by a psychiatrist who was not aware of which of the two types of family the child came from, twice as many were diagnosed with depression.[19] Although depression was the most common disorder among these children, other problems were also found, the most common of which were anxiety and impaired attention. Ten years later, the children of depressed parents were found to be three times more likely than children from families where neither parent had depression to suffer from depression and phobias, and five times more likely to be dependent on alcohol. They also reported more problems with work, marriage and family life.[20]

These findings are not unusual. In a different investigation, almost half of the children with a depressed parent were diagnosed with depression themselves, 37 per cent with behaviour disorders including aggression and attention difficulties, and 32 per cent with emotional disorders such as anxiety.[21] These diagnoses were not mutually exclusive; many of the children had more than one disorder. Another study found 41 per cent of children of depressed parents to have at least one psychiatric disorder compared with 15 per cent of children whose parents were not depressed, and 33 per cent of the children of depressed parents had received treatment for their own emotional or behavioural problems, whereas this was true of only 9 per cent of the other children. Moreover, 3 per cent had been hospitalised because of their psychological difficulties, 7 per cent had received medication, and 5 per cent had attempted suicide. In contrast, none of the children of parents who were well had attempted to kill themselves or had needed hospital or drug treatment.[22] Having a parent who is depressed, it seems, places children at risk not only for depression but for other disorders as well.

It is perhaps not surprising that depression in parents is associated with psychological problems in children. The question of most interest to psychologists is how this comes about. One explanation is that being depressed reduces the ability to be an effective parent.[23] Just as we saw with marital conflict, depression is thought to interfere with parents' control and discipline of their children, and also with their emotional availability and sensitivity to them, thus jeopardising children's security of attachment.

A number of studies have shown that depressed parents tend either to be very lenient when it comes to monitoring and disciplining their children's behaviour, or very authoritarian, often switching between the two. When mothers and their pre-school children were observed together to examine how they controlled their children's behaviour, depressed mothers were more likely than other mothers to give in to the child and were less likely to negotiate a compromise.[24] It seemed that more effort was needed to reach a mutually agreeable resolution than depressed mothers could muster and that they gave in to unreasonable demands from their children as an easy way out.

Because people who are depressed often look sad, appear to be wrapped up in their own thoughts and tend not to be very talkative or affectionate – exactly the opposite characteristics to those which are important for children's development of secure attachment relationships – the attachments of children whose mothers are depressed have received considerable attention. There is certainly evidence that mothers who are depressed behave differently with their children than mothers who are not.[25] Detailed analyses of video-recordings of mothers interacting with their babies show that, compared with other mothers, depressed mothers are less warm and less responsive. They can also be more critical, intrusive and hostile. Unlike mothers who are not depressed, they do not use exaggerated facial expressions or tones of voice when talking to their infants, and with toddlers they use fewer explanations, suggestions and questions. When depressed and non-depressed mothers were observed playing with their 1- and 2-year-olds, depressed mothers and their children were found to be less co-ordinated with each other. A close examination of the interactions showed that mothers who were not depressed tended to adjust their behaviour to that of their children; if the child switched attention to another activity, the mother would follow suit. Depressed mothers were less likely to do this, and they and their children withdrew more frequently into their own separate worlds.[26]

When mothers are depressed, their unstimulating and unresponsive behaviour is reflected in their babies who also seem depressed. These babies are more withdrawn, less active, more irritable and smile less often than other babies. Interestingly, when mothers who are not depressed are asked to 'act depressed', their babies immediately become distressed and look away, showing that a mother's behaviour towards her infant has a profound effect on the infant's emotional state. It is not just with their depressed mother that babies seem withdrawn. They also appear less happy and less active when interacting with other adults, and can even cause non-depressed adults to act in a less animated and enthusiastic way towards them.[27]

Does the less responsive behaviour of depressed mothers mean that their children will be insecurely attached? It seems that it does. Studies that have directly examined the link between maternal depression and insecure attachment in children have established a link between the two. When Lynne Murray classified 18-month-old children as securely or insecurely attached according to their response to the Strange Situation Test (described in Chapter 5), she found two-thirds of children of depressed mothers to be insecurely attached compared with only one-third of children whose mothers were well.[28] Marian Radke-Yarrow and her colleagues also compared Strange Situation Test classifications of children of severely depressed mothers with those of children of mothers with mild depression and children whose mothers were not depressed. Fifty-five per cent of the children whose mothers were severely depressed were insecurely attached, whereas this was true of less than 30 per cent of each of the other two groups of children.[29] A rate of insecure attachment of around 30 per cent is what would be expected among well parents and their children.

It has been suggested that not only does parental depression lead to insecure attachments in children but that insecure attachment may itself be a first step towards children becoming depressed. As discussed in Chapter 5, through their relationships with parents children are believed to develop internal working models of themselves as lovable (in the case of securely attached children) or as unworthy of being loved (in the case of insecurely attached children). It is these very feelings of low self-esteem experienced by insecurely attached children that are also characteristic of children who become depressed. Only when children who have experienced a poor relationship with their depressed parents are followed up to adulthood will we know to what extent the parenting problems of their childhood contribute towards psychological difficulties later in life.

Another explanation for the behavioural and emotional problems of children of depressed parents is that it is the greater marital conflict in couples where one partner is depressed, rather than the depression itself, that is responsible. We know that marital conflict is associated with difficulties for children. We also know that depression and marital conflict often go hand in hand. It is possible, therefore, that the problems experienced by children of depressed parents result from marital conflict rather than the depression itself.

The fact that marital conflict is associated with the problems experienced by children of depressed parents has been demonstrated in a number of studies. For example, in an investigation of the relationship between parental depression, marital discord and children's behaviour at school, children's disruptive, impatient and aggressive behaviour in the classroom was largely accounted for by hostility between the parents rather than the parents' depression; children of depressed parents who were not in conflict were no more likely than children of well parents to show behaviour problems at school.[30] In another study of mothers' responsiveness towards their 2-year-olds, the quality of the relationship between the mother and child was more closely associated with the state of the parents' marriage than the mother's psychiatric condition.[31]

But whether marital conflict, on its own, can account for the psychological difficulties experienced by children of depressed parents remains an open question. In their review of all relevant studies, Geraldine Downey and James Coyne concluded that marital discord was linked to conduct problems in children of depressed parents such as aggression and disruptive behaviour, but that it could not explain the high rates of childhood depression.[32] They believe that marital conflict in families with a depressed parent increases children's risk for conduct problems whereas it is the parents' depression, not the associated marital discord, that increases children's own risk for depression. It seems most likely that marital conflict is one of several pathways through which parental depression can lead to childhood disorder. As marital conflict is both a cause and a consequence of depression in adults a complex relationship may exist between the two. Not only can depression cause marital conflict but marital conflict can also cause depression.

To further complicate the issue, depression and marital conflict may each be caused by external factors, and these external factors may, in themselves, be implicated in children's development of psychological problems. Depressed parents and their children are often exposed to a range of difficulties including financial hardship, poor housing and lack of social support. These stressors not only increase the risk of both depression and marital conflict in parents but also, as we shall see in Chapter 7, pose a direct threat to the psychological adjustment of children.

Although it is generally assumed that depression in parents causes psychological problems in children rather than the other way around, the possibility that children can cause, or at least contribute towards, depression in their parents cannot be dismissed. Just as difficult children may exacerbate marital conflict, so might they be involved in the development or maintenance of parental depression. A mother who is depressed, for example, may become even more depressed by her failure to manage a difficult child, thus increasing her depression. It is not easy to determine what comes first, children's problem behaviour or maternal depression, as children of depressed mothers behave differently from other children even in the first few months of life. Researchers who have attempted to tease apart the separate influences of the mother and the child have concluded that the relationship between the two is a complex one. Both parties, it seems, play a part.

Another explanation for the high incidence of psychological problems among children of depressed parents is that the children's disorders are not a consequence of their parents' behaviour but instead are inherited.[33] The fact that depression, as opposed to any other disorder, is the most common psychiatric problem experienced by children of depressed parents lends weight to this view. Evidence in support of the genetic transmission of depression from parents to children comes from studies showing that immediate relatives of depressed people have a greater than average risk of developing depression themselves. Although this finding may be explained by the effects of growing up in the same family, it may also result from an inherited vulnerability to become depressed. Even stronger evidence comes from twin studies that show a greater likelihood of identical twins both having depression than non-identical twins, again indicating that depression is an inherited disorder. But just because one identical twin is depressed does not necessarily mean that the other will be depressed as well. In only about half of identical twin pairs where one twin has depression will the other twin also have depression. The fact that one identical twin may be depressed and the other not tells us that the development of depression cannot be explained by genetic factors alone.

What these findings suggest is that some people are genetically predisposed to become depressed whereas others are not. But whether or not we actually develop depression will depend not just on our genetic makeup but on our experiences as well. Someone who is genetically vulnerable may remain free of depression whereas others with no genetic predisposition may suffer from depression throughout their lives.

We might expect that children of schizophrenic parents are even more prone to develop psychological problems than children whose parents are depressed. The hallucinations and delusions that are a feature of this disorder, together with bizarre behaviour and changes in mood, are likely to produce a disrupted family environment in which to grow up. Several investigations have looked at the development of children with schizophrenic parents in comparison with children whose parents do not have a psychiatric disorder. The Stony Brook High-Risk Project studied eighty school-age children with a schizophrenic parent and found them to have reduced intellectual ability, poor attention and difficulties in social relationships.[34] Similarly, the Emory University Project, which focused on preschool children, found schizophrenic mothers to be withdrawn and emotionally uninvolved with their children, and the children to perform poorly in tests of intellectual functioning and to have poor social skills.[35]

But studies that have compared families with a schizophrenic parent with families with a depressed parent have failed to find marked differences between the children.[32] Although the children of schizophrenic parents tend to have the most severe problems, in many ways they do not differ from the children of depressed parents. It seems that having a parent with a psychiatric disorder produces difficulties for children but that having a schizophrenic parent is not necessarily worse for children than having a parent who is depressed.

Children of schizophrenic parents were originally investigated to assess their risk of developing the disorder themselves. Although by late adolescence or early adulthood many do have psychiatric problems, not all have schizophrenia. The Stony Brook High-Risk Project found 23 per cent of young adult children of schizophrenic parents to have a diagnosable psychiatric disorder compared with 10 per cent of a comparison group of young adults with well parents, and an even higher proportion of children of schizophrenic parents had more general difficulties in social functioning.[34] A similar outcome was found in the New York High-Risk Project with around one-third of the young adults who had two schizophrenic parents developing schizophrenia or a similar disorder themselves.[36]

Although these studies cannot tell us about the relative importance of genes and the environment in the onset of schizophrenia in the children of affected parents, it is known from studies of identical and non-identical twins, and from studies of adopted children of schizophrenic parents who show a high incidence of schizophrenia despite being raised apart from their schizophrenic parents, that there is a genetic component to the development of this disorder. A study in Finland has attempted to assess the contribution of both genes and the environment by studying children of schizophrenic parents who had been adopted by well parents.[37] The researchers found that disturbed relationships in the adoptive families increased the likelihood of these children developing disorders connected with schizophrenia. Although there were two few cases of schizophrenia to study schizophrenia itself, the findings suggest that aspects of the family environment may increase or decrease the risk of schizophrenia in children who have a genetic vulnerability to the disorder.

Children whose parents are dependent on alcohol or drugs are also at a disadvantage.[38] Compared with other children they are more likely to show conduct problems including antisocial behaviour and delinquency. An obvious explanation is that parents who are often drunk or drugged, or whose attention is focused on obtaining their next supply, cannot properly care for their children. But this is not the only reason why these children are at risk. People who become dependent on alcohol, or on addictive drugs such as heroin or cocaine, often live in conditions of extreme poverty. They may also suffer from a psychiatric disorder such as depression, which, as we have already seen, is associated with the development of psychological problems in children.

A high rate of neglect and abuse has been found among the children of alcoholic and drug-addicted parents. It is not unusual for these children to grow up in an atmosphere of threat and violence, and many end up living apart from their mother either with other family members or with foster- or adoptive parents. A study that followed up babies born to mothers on heroin found that half were living elsewhere by the time they were a year old.[39] In addition to the life experiences that place these children at risk for psychological problems, they may inherit a vulnerability towards alcohol or drug dependence themselves. The adult sons of alcoholic fathers, for example, are three times more likely to also be alcoholic than the sons of fathers who are not dependent on alcohol.[40] Although they may be influenced by growing up with an alcoholic father, twin and adoption studies have shown that genetic factors are also involved.

For children whose mothers consume large amounts of alcohol or drugs during pregnancy there are additional risks.[38] In addition to their reduced birthweight, many babies of alcoholic mothers show delayed development in infancy, as well as intellectual impairment, hyperactivity and difficulty in concentration throughout their childhood and adolescent years. Infants whose mothers are dependent on heroin are born addicted to this drug. Not only do these new-borns experience unpleasant withdrawal symptoms beginning in their first days of life, but they may also suffer from long-lasting effects such as poor physical co-ordination, poor attention and hyperactivity as they grow up. The effects of prenatal exposure to cocaine are less clear-cut, although there is growing evidence that babies whose mothers took cocaine during pregnancy are slower to develop, particularly in their co-ordination of movement.[41]

We cannot be certain whether the problems experienced by school-age children whose mothers were addicted to alcohol or drugs during pregnancy result from their exposure to these substances in the womb or from being raised by an addicted parent. Once again, it seems most likely that several factors contribute towards the difficulties of these children, not least because prenatal exposure to alcohol or drugs makes infants difficult to handle which, in turn, results in less sensitive and responsive parenting by drug- or alcohol-dependent parents who may have difficulty in coping with even the easiest of babies. Investigations of the ways in which addicted mothers interact with their infants have shown them to be less involved and more hostile than other mothers. Not surprisingly, it has also been found that infants of addicted mothers are more likely to be insecurely attached.[38]

Thus it seems that parents' marital and psychological problems can have marked and long-lasting effects on the psychological adjustment of their children. Although the impact on children is partly dependent on the extent to which the parents' difficulties interfere with their relationship with the child, even when this relationship remains good, children are placed at risk as a result of their exposure to the parents' disturbed state.

But most children do not live alone with their parents; they have brothers and sisters as well. And the relationships they form with their siblings can either augment or diminish the impact of poor parenting in families under stress. We know from our own experience that some siblings usually get on well while others always seem to be fighting, and yet others are friendly one minute and in conflict the next. Why is it that pairs of siblings can be so different?

One reason seems to be that temperament plays a part. Children who generally tend to be hostile and aggressive are more likely to have conflictual relationships with their siblings, and if one sibling is hostile and aggressive the more likely it is that the other will be as well. Parents also influence the quality of relationships that brothers and sisters form with each other. The research of Judy Dunn and others has shown that parents who treat their children differently, favouring one over the other, are more likely to have children who do not get on.[42] Although we cannot assume that the differential treatment by parents *causes* conflict between their children (the siblings' behaviour could cause the parents to treat them differently), the finding that the 'favourite' child is less likely to develop psychological problems than his or her sibling points to the potentially far-reaching effects of parents' preferential behaviour towards an individual child.

It is not just by treating their children differently that parents influence how siblings relate to each other. The quality of their own relationship seems to have a direct impact on the quality of relationships among their children.[43] Conflict between parents, or parental divorce, is often accompanied by an increase in hostility between children in the family. But this is not always the case. Siblings can also support each other when the family is in difficulty. In homes with unhappy marriages, it seems that children have fewer problems if they have good relationships with their brothers and sisters.[44] By confiding in each other, and giving and receiving comfort, they can help each other cope in times of stress.

But it is not just what happens within the family that matters for children. Experiences in the wider social world also make a difference, and it is to these that we turn in Chapter 7.

Chapter 7

Children's individual characteristics and their wider social world

For many children, their first experience of life beyond the family is of day-care. Now that it is usual for mothers to work outside the home, most children are looked after by someone else for part of the day, often by a person who is paid to do so, and many attend day-care centres.

Research on the effects of day-care on children has tended to address the question of 'What are the harmful effects?' rather than 'How do children benefit from this experience?', and has focused on the two areas of child development thought to be at risk – emotional well-being and intellectual functioning. It has traditionally been assumed that it is optimal for young children to stay at home with their mother, and that whatever arrangements are made to allow a mother to go out to work will be second-best for the child. More recently, attention has turned from the general question of the effects of day-care on children to consideration of the importance of the quality of day-care that children receive, as well as the influence of the child's family background. Although good-quality day-care comes in a variety of forms, the presence of warm, responsive and highly trained caregivers who are responsible for small groups of children is thought to be essential.[1,2]

Probably the most commonly voiced concern about the emotional well-being of children in day-care is that daily separations from their mother will jeopardise the security of their attachment to her. It is not just childcare professionals who see this as a potential problem; mothers worry about it as well. Particularly when tired after a hard day's work, and not as responsive and available to their children as they would like, it is a nagging concern for many working mothers that their children will end up feeling closer to their day-care teacher than to them. In fact, research has shown that this is not the case.[3,4]

Most studies that have examined the security of attachment of children of working mothers have compared the attachment classifications of children in day-care with those of children who remained with their mother at home. The Strange Situation Test (described in Chapter 5) has generally been used to assess attachment. From the early research it appeared that children in day-care were indeed more likely to be insecurely attached to their mother than children of mothers who were not employed. Taking all the studies together, it was estimated that around 40 per cent of children in day-care were insecurely attached compared with less than 30 per cent of children whose mothers remained at home, and that insecure attachment was most likely among babies who spent at least twenty hours a week in day-care in their first year of life.[5]

Not surprisingly, these findings were highly controversial, the implication being that mothers of young babies should not go out to work. However, critics pointed out that the main difference between infants who attended day-care and those who did not was in insecure-avoidant rather than insecure-resistant attachment. As insecure-avoidant attachment is characterised by the failure to approach the mother after a period of separation, it was argued that children who attend day-care are used to daily separations from their mother and may not approach her when she returns from work because they are comfortable with this situation and not because they are insecurely attached to her.[6] Moreover, 60 per cent of babies who spent at least half of each day in day-care *were* securely attached to their mother, with only a slightly higher proportion of those in day-care than those who were cared for at home classified as insecurely attached.

In an attempt to settle the issue, the Institute of Health and Human Development in the United States launched a study of more than a thousand families in 1991.[7] Not only has a large number of families been studied from ten different geographical locations but this investigation also has the advantage of including many different types of childcare arrangements (e.g. nurseries, childminders and grandparents), as well as information about each family, so that the effects of childcare can be determined after taking account of other factors that may influence children's development.

To assess security of attachment to their mother, the children took part in a Strange Situation Test when they were 15 months old. It was found that being cared for by someone other than the mother before their first birthday, even for substantial periods of time, did not, in itself, result in an increased number of insecurely attached babies when family characteristics were taken into account. However, poor-quality childcare, more than ten hours per week of childcare, and experiencing several changes in childcare arrangements in the first fifteen months of life each increased the proportion of insecurely attached infants when combined with insensitive and unresponsive parenting by the mother. So it seems that inadequate and extensive childcare can increase the risk of insecure attachment but only among babies who are not protected by a good relationship with their mother.

In terms of children's intellectual development, researchers have moved away from the rather simplistic question of whether day-care is good or bad for children to the issue of whether the quality of day-care makes a difference. From the findings of a number of studies of day-care settings of varying quality in different geographical locations, it seems that it does. In Bermuda, where a high proportion of children are in day-care, Kathleen McCartney found that 3- to 5-year-old children whose caregivers frequently talked to them had better language skills than children from poorer quality day-care.[8] They were also more sociable than their peers, and more considerate of others.[9] The large-scale investigation by the Institute of Health and Human Development has confirmed these findings, once again demonstrating that the more that caregivers talk to and listen to children, the more advanced is their language and intellectual development, and the readier they are for school by the age of 3.[10] So the concern that children in day-care would be at a disadvantage compared with their peers whose mothers remained at home appears to be unfounded for children in high-quality care. If anything, their intellectual ability and development of language are enhanced by their experience.

Both of these studies took into consideration aspects of the children's family background that might affect their development. For this reason we can be confident that the differences identified between children are related to the quality of childcare, and not to family factors. This is important because children's intellectual and language development is affected by their family circumstances and so the differences between children in good- and poor-quality day-care may have more to do with their family background than with the type of day-care they experience. Mothers who have financial problems, for example, may spend less time playing with or reading to their children at home, and this lack of stimulation at home, rather than poor-quality day-care, may cause children to fall behind.

Although these studies found the quality of day-care to influence children's intellectual and language development independently of their family circumstances, children's experiences at home were more predictive of their performance than the quality of day-care. The intellectual and language development of children in day-care is therefore dependent not only on what happens in day-care but also on what happens at home. There is also a greater likelihood of children from disadvantaged family backgrounds being placed in poor-quality day-care, thus reducing their potential to do well. For this reason, a number of projects have been set up specifically to compensate for the impoverished home lives of children from disadvantaged families. This type of intervention, focusing on learning, providing emotional support and generally enriching children's lives, has proved to be successful in improving children's intellectual and social development.[11]

Although it seems that good-quality day-care does not cause immediate difficulties for children, perhaps the negative effects only become apparent later on. It seems not. Researchers who have followed up children who attended day-care in their pre-school years have found no adverse effects on their emotional or intellectual development as they grow up.[12,13] Even children who were exposed to poor-quality care seem to show no long-lasting effects, and children from disadvantaged backgrounds who were in high-quality care often benefit from the experience.[11]

As children move from day-care into school, they spend a growing amount of time with other children, and these other children soon become an important influence in their lives. Through their relationships with peers, children learn how to get along with others; how to deal with conflict, how to share and how to communicate are just some of the skills children acquire through their daily interactions with their peers.

But not all children are popular with other children, and being disliked not only interferes with learning about social relationships but can also have a profound effect on how they feel about themselves. Children may be unpopular in different ways. Some are actively disliked by their peers and rejected by them. Others are neglected but not especially disliked.

Researchers interested in the experiences of unpopular children devised a technique for assessing whether a child is liked or disliked.[14] All children in a class are asked to write down, in confidence, the names of the three children they like best, and the three children they like least. By adding up the number of times each child is nominated as being liked or disliked, it is possible to calculate who are the most popular and who the least popular children in the class. The ways in which popular and unpopular children differ from each other can then be explored.

So what is it that makes children unpopular with their peers? It seems that children who are rejected are less fun to be with than children who are liked.[15] In particular, they are more aggressive, disruptive and bossy than popular children. Neglected children are not aggressive. Instead, they tend to be shy and avoid other children, and often play alone.

But is it their antisocial behaviour that makes them disliked, or is it because they are disliked that they behave this way? Simply comparing popular and unpopular children does not answer the question because it does not tell us which comes first. One way of overcoming this problem has been to study groups of children who do not know each other. Because they have never met, it is possible to find out whether children who are unpopular with their peers are also unpopular with a completely new group of children, and what it is about their behaviour that causes them to be disliked. These studies tell us that it is how children behave in social situations that determines whether or not they will be accepted by their peers. Once again, it was aggressive children who were most often disliked.[16,17] Although it is possible that children who were aggressive in this situation behaved aggressively because they were used to being rejected, it seems that whatever the reason for their aggression, other children disliked them for it.

But not all aggressive children are unpopular with their peers. On the contrary, some are very popular. Jennifer Parkhurst and Steven Asher asked 450 teenagers to complete a questionnaire about their peer relationships, and found that aggressive children who were liked had redeeming features as well.[18] Many were good at sports, fun to play with and seen as good leaders.

The negative effects on children of being rejected can be profound and long-lasting, often beginning in the very early years. When the peer relationships of children entering kindergarten were examined, those who were rejected within the first two months were most likely to dislike school, avoid school and perform poorly at school by the end of their first year.[19] Older children are also affected. In a study of 7- to 12-year-olds, those who were rejected by their peers were again more likely to have behaviour problems and less likely to achieve good grades.[20] In the long term, rejected children are more likely than their peers to become delinquent, develop psychological problems and drop out of school.[21,22] Rejected children, it seems, stay rejected as they grow up. Whereas rejected children who are aggressive may become delinquent, rejected children who are not aggressive are most likely to remain socially withdrawn. The outcomes for neglected children are less bleak, but to the extent that they experience difficulties later in life, it seems that they are more likely to have emotional than behavioural problems.

Just because children are unpopular does not mean that they do not have any friends. Although being popular and having friends usually go hand in hand, Jeffrey Parker and Steven Asher found that nearly half of the unpopular children whom they studied had a best friend, while some of the very popular children did not.[23] Although some children seem not to mind not having friends, most feel lonely as a result. But it would be wrong to assume that having friends is always good, and not having friends is bad. It is true that children who have friends are more sociable, have higher self-esteem and are less likely to experience emotional problems. However, it is not clear whether having friends causes children to feel good about themselves, or whether children who feel good about themselves are more likely to have friends.

Who the child's friends are also makes a difference. Not surprisingly, having a best friend who is always in trouble increases a child's chances of getting into trouble as well. But it is not simply a case of some children being a bad influence on others. Children are more likely to make friends in the first place with children who are like themselves.[24] Children who don't like school, or who like sports, or who drink alcohol or take drugs, are attracted to other children who are the same, and once children make friends their shared interests make them more similar as time goes on. So getting into trouble becomes even more likely when children become friends with other children who are just like them.

Although children's experiences within their peer group take on a greater significance as they grow up, relationships with their peers cannot be entirely divorced from relationships with their parents. Parents influence children's social lives in several ways. As Ross Parke and Gary Ladd point out, how parents interact with their children has an indirect effect on how children interact with their peers; children who have positive interactions with their parents, especially during play, are more likely to be popular with their peers.[25] One explanation is that positive interaction with parents allows children to develop a good understanding of other people's emotions, as well as appropriate ways of responding to different emotions, which they carry over into the peer group. Secure attachment to parents is also associated with good relationships with other children. We cannot be certain, however, whether secure attachment to parents actually causes children to be accepted by their peers.

Parents may also have a direct influence on their children's interactions with peers by guiding them in how to conduct these relationships, although the involvement of parents may not always be good for the child. As their children grow older, the extent to which parents monitor their children's social activities becomes important. The research of Gerald Patterson and his colleagues has shown that the parents of children who get into trouble fail to monitor their children's activities.[26,27] Often they do not know where their children are or who they are with. A further role of parents is the management of their children's social lives. Whether children play with other children, particularly when they are young, may depend on whether their parents give them the opportunity.

The environment in which children grow up also has a major impact on their lives. Children raised in poverty, in comparison with children from affluent homes, are more likely to perform poorly at school, drop out of school early, become involved in delinquent and criminal behaviour, have unwanted pregnancies and develop emotional problems in their teenage years.[28] Poverty interferes with children's psychological development in many ways. Even before birth, poor children are at a disadvantage: they are more likely to be exposed to drugs, alcohol, nicotine and malnutrition in the womb, and to be born prematurely. As they grow up they are less likely to go to good schools and to have access to toys and books at home, both of which mitigate against high academic achievement. But most importantly, poverty has a pervasive and damaging effect on the quality of parenting that children receive. Parents who are faced with the pressures of economic hardship often become depressed, their marriages deteriorate, and the demands of their children become a further source of stress.

This finding was clearly demonstrated in a study of almost four hundred children in the rural Midwest of the United States. In the 1980s, this area suffered a serious economic crisis. Thousands of farmers and small businesses lost their means of livelihood with devastating effects on family life. A chain of events that began with an economic crisis ended in an increase in antisocial and aggressive behaviour among the children of the area. Rand Conger, Glen Elder and colleagues found not only that these children were exposed to increased marital conflict and psychological distress which, as we saw in Chapter 6, are both related to the development of psychological problems in children, but also that their parents were more hostile in their interactions with them.[29,30] The children's difficulties were found to be a direct consequence of the deterioration in their relationship with their parents, which stemmed from their parents' hostility towards each other and their psychological distress.

Similar findings were reported in a comparison of delinquent and non-delinquent city children in a study by Robert Sampson and John Laub designed to answer the question of why some boys raised in poor neighbourhoods became delinquent and others did not.[31] The link between poverty and delinquency was found to be mediated to a large extent through parents' inability to discipline their children effectively. Parents who were unable to control their children and who punished them in a harsh and rejecting manner were most likely to have delinquent adolescents, whereas parents who monitored their children's activities and disciplined them in such a way that the child still felt loved and accepted were less likely to have a delinquent child even when they lived in conditions of extreme economic disadvantage. It seems, therefore, that poverty does generate delinquency, and that the link between the two results, in part at least, from the insidious effects that poverty has on family life. Hostility is high in these families, not just between the parents but also between the parents and the child.

But not all children raised under even the most extreme conditions of social disadvantage grow up to be disturbed adults. We sometimes hear of highly successful people coming from violent, abusive or impoverished family backgrounds from which they managed to escape. Why is it that some children are able to overcome early adversity whereas other children become so badly affected that their early experiences continue to have a destructive influence on their psychological well-being throughout their lives?

One answer to this question is that some children are more resilient than others.[32,33] They seem to be much less affected by the kinds of stresses that for other children would lead to psychological problems. They may experience their parents' divorce, or be raised in conditions of extreme poverty, or they may even be the victims of abuse, but however bad their experiences they always seem to bounce back. What is it that is different about these children?

One of the first studies to address the question of why some children succumb to pressure and others do not was carried out by Emmy Werner and her colleagues on a Hawaiian island where many children were being raised under extreme hardship.[34] All of the children born in a one-year period, around six hundred babies in total, were followed up when they were 2, 10, 18 and 32 years old to find out what happened to them as they grew up. Approximately two hundred of the children were classified as 'high risk', meaning that they were vulnerable to the development of psychological problems because of their childhood experiences; they had birth complications, were born into poverty, had an unstable family life and one or both parents had a psychiatric disorder. In spite of their difficult childhood, one-third of the high-risk children were found to be well-adjusted and confident adults. However difficult their upbringing, it was not inevitable that these children developed psychological problems, not even those who were at greatest risk.

So how did the resilient children compare with those who did develop serious psychological problems? It seems that they were different right from the start. As babies they were more affectionate, more active, and had fewer eating and sleeping problems. At school they were higher achievers, more independent, had more interests and got on well with their peers. They also had higher self-esteem and felt in greater control of their lives, and they were more likely to be girls. But it was not just these children's own characteristics that set them apart. A further difference between them was that the resilient children were more likely to have a close and affectionate relationship with at least one parent or parent-figure. They also received emotional support from outside the family, perhaps from a teacher or other interested adult. Having a warm and supportive relationship with at least one person was found to be an important factor in protecting vulnerable children from the adverse effects of the stressors in their lives.

So it seems that children are protected both by their own characteristics and by close relationships with others. The two are, of course, related. Parents who themselves are under high levels of stress will find it easier to be warm and supportive towards an easy child than a difficult one. Whatever the type of adversity studied in more recent investigations, be it poverty, divorce, abuse or a parent's psychiatric disorder, the factors associated with resilience have been strikingly similar to those originally identified in Hawaii.[32,33]

Even as new-borns, infants show different characteristics from each other. Some cry more than others, some are more active than others, and some like being cuddled whereas others do not. It was Alexander Thomas, Stella Chess and colleagues in the 1960s who were the first to study differences in the behaviour of new-born babies.[35] They showed that early in infancy, babies could be classified as easy, difficult or slow to warm up. Easy babies were in a good mood most of the time, adapted well to new experiences and showed regular patterns of eating and sleeping. In contrast, difficult babies were irritable, reacted badly to new situations, and showed irregular eating and sleeping habits. Those classified as slow to warm up took time to adapt to changes in their routine.

More recently, researchers have come up with a variety of ways in which new-born infants differ from each other. Although they do not all agree about which are the most important or the most interesting, there is general consensus that infants do differ in temperament right from birth.[36,37] Key differences include how active the baby is, how easily the baby becomes distressed or frightened, how irritable the baby is, the ease with which the baby responds to new situations, and the extent to which the baby likes being with people and expresses enjoyment by smiling or appearing content.

Because babies show differences in temperament from early on in life, it is assumed that they are born with these characteristics; but the child's experiences are also thought to play a part.[36,37] Whether or not a child becomes upset in a new situation will depend not only on that child's tendency to become distressed but also on what usually happens when he or she cries for help. If the mother or caretaker is quick to respond and is able to provide comfort, the baby will be less likely to continue to show distress. If no comfort is forthcoming then the baby's distress will be more likely to persist. But the child's temperament will also affect how people respond to the child. A mother may be more likely to pick up a crying baby who is easily soothed than a baby who continues to cry whatever she tries to do to help. A baby's temperament can have a profound effect on the behaviour of the key people in his or her life.

So the relationship between a child's temperament and how other people respond to that child is complex. It may be that characteristics of the child cause the mother to behave in certain ways, or the mother's behaviour towards the child may encourage or discourage particular characteristics in the child. Most likely, both processes are operating so that the mother's relationship with the child is influenced by her child's temperament, and her child's temperament is influenced to some extent by his or her relationship with the mother. We have already seen in Chapter 5 that this seems to be the case in relation to attachment; infants with difficult temperaments are thought to be less likely to form secure attachments than easy infants because their mothers are less likely to respond sensitively towards them.

The issue of whether our behaviour from birth onwards is a product of our genes or our environment, known as the 'nature–nurture' debate, has been one of the most contentious issues in behavioural science. One way of investigating this question has been to compare the similarities between identical and non-identical twins, i.e. to establish whether identical twins are more similar to each other in their behaviour than non-identical twins. The rationale for this approach is that identical twins have identical genes whereas the genes of non-identical twins are no more alike than those of ordinary siblings. Thus if identical twins are more similar to each other than non-identical twins with respect to a particular characteristic, this indicates that the characteristic under investigation is determined by genes. We know that identical twins look alike because they have the same genetic makeup; but does their identical genetic makeup cause them to behave alike as well?

What the findings of twin studies show is that differences in personality, IQ and some psychological disorders such as schizophrenia, manic depression and autism are to some extent caused by differences in genetic makeup.[38,39] Identical twins are more similar in these characteristics than non-identical twins. Interestingly, however, identical twins do not always show the same behaviours. This tells us that environmental influences also play a part. For example, an identical twin of a person who is schizophrenic is more likely also to be schizophrenic than a non-identical twin, but not all identical twins of schizophrenics will become schizophrenic themselves. This means that whether or not an individual will develop schizophrenia depends not only on his or her genetic makeup but on environmental factors as well. As the behavioural geneticist Robert Plomin points out, genetic research provides us with the best evidence for the importance of non-genetic effects on development.[38,39] The fact that genetically identical twins show different behaviour means that our behaviour is not determined solely by our genes. In fact, for most psychological characteristics, it seems that environmental factors play an important part.

These days, the question of interest to behavioural researchers is no longer 'Is this characteristic genetically or environmentally determined?' but instead 'How do genes and the environment interact to produce this characteristic?'[40,41,42] It is now believed that what we inherit is a predisposition to behave in certain ways, and that our experiences in the environment in which we live will either minimise or maximise our inherited potential.

Parents may influence children's behaviour not only by passing on genes but also by creating a family environment influenced by their own genetic makeup. Genetically influenced psychiatric disorder in parents, for example, may result in increased marital conflict which, in turn, may have an adverse effect on the well-being of the child. Moreover, the child's genetically influenced behaviour may affect the behaviour of others towards the child, or may result in the child seeking out particular environments. Thus children with a genetic predisposition to engage in illegal activities such as drug taking or theft may be rejected by their parents, and may be attracted to other children who do the same as them, making them even more likely to continue their illegal acts. In addition, genes increase a person's susceptibility to particular environmental risks. Whereas a child with no genetic risk may not suffer the negative consequences of an adverse environment, a different child with a high genetic risk may be more sensitive to environmental effects. In this way, a child with a genetic disposition towards behavioural problems may be more likely to develop such problems when faced with a hostile family environment than a child in a similar family environment who does not carry the genetic risk.

Another method for establishing the relative contribution of genes and the environment to the development of certain behaviours has been to examine the similarities of siblings who have been adopted into different families in comparison with the similarities of siblings who have been raised by their biological parents.[43] By separating the effects of nature from the effects of nurture, these studies tell us whether resemblance between siblings is due to shared genes or shared family environment. If siblings reared together are more similar than siblings reared apart, this tells us that the characteristics they have in common are more influenced by their shared family environment than their shared genes. If shared genes are responsible, the siblings would be just as likely to show the same characteristics whether or not they were raised in the same family environment. What these studies show, once again, is that most psychological characteristics are influenced by both genes and the environment.

In a further attempt to establish the extent to which resemblance among siblings is derived from their shared environment as opposed to their shared genetic makeup, behavioural geneticists have also examined children of different biological parents adopted into the same family. Any similarities between these genetically unrelated adoptive siblings could only be due to their shared family environment and not to their shared genes. It is possible not only to determine the extent to which the behavioural characteristics they have in common result from their shared environment but also to establish the extent to which the differences in their behaviour result from differences in their environment. In spite of growing up in the same home, these children were found not to resemble each other with respect to their psychological characteristics. It was this way of looking at environmental effects on psychological development that led Robert Plomin and his colleagues to come up with a surprising result – the environmental influences that shape children's development are different for children in the same family.[38,39,44]

This finding has changed our understanding of how families influence children. It used to be believed that children in the same family were exposed to the same environment. For this reason, family influences could not explain why children in the same family turned out differently. Whether their parents had a happy marriage or were in conflict, and whether their parents were psychologically stable or disturbed, were circumstances that were assumed to affect all children in the family equally. Differences between siblings were thought to result from differences in their genetic makeup, not differences in their family environment. It now seems that this assumption was wrong. Although children may be exposed to an identical family environment, the impact of that environment may differ dramatically for each child. Robert Plomin argues that it is the environmental influences specific to an individual child, rather than those common to all children in the family, that are most important in shaping children's development. Although there is disagreement about the relative importance of these two processes, the unique environmental influences help explain why children in the same family can be so different.

For example, a mother may be more affectionate towards one child than another, and the fact that a mother treats her two children differently may stem from differences in their behaviour towards her. One baby may like to be kissed and cuddled a lot whereas the other may wriggle out of any close physical contact. We have already seen that a child's temperament can influence the behaviour of the mother. In this way, two siblings may experience quite different relationships with their mother because of differences in their behaviour towards her. Evidence that children in the same family do have different experiences comes from studies of siblings' perceptions of their relationships with parents.[45] Siblings commonly report differential treatment by their parents such that one child is perceived to be 'the favourite'. Although this can create difficulties between them, whether or not tensions will arise seems to depend on whether the parents' behaviour is seen as fair.

What can we conclude from this research? One thing is clear. In considering how families affect children, we can no longer assume that just because children grow up in the same family they will have identical experiences. A much loved child may share a home with a less valued brother or sister, and their relationship with their parents may have little in common. Changes in family life may also impact differently on one sibling than another. The parents' divorce may be devastating to one child while the other may come through it relatively unharmed. But this does not mean that experiences that are common to all children in the family do not matter. Shared family experiences can also have an important influence on the child.[40,41]

Whether children's experience of growing up in their particular family promotes psychological adjustment or produces psychological problems depends not just on the quality of parenting they experience or on the characteristics of the child. Instead, each will influence the other in complex ways that may be quite different from one sibling to another. We must also remember that children and parents do not live in isolation. The wider social world will not only influence how family members see themselves but will also affect the nature of their relationships with each other.

Chapter 8

Parenting
What really counts?

As we enter the twenty-first century, the idealised family unit of a heterosexual couple in a stable marriage with naturally conceived children is becoming increasingly rare. Indeed, since the birth of the first 'test-tube' baby, Louise Brown, in 1978 it has become possible for a child to have five parents – an egg donor, a sperm donor, a surrogate mother who hosts the pregnancy, and the two social parents who are the child's mum and dad. And yet, for the sake of our children, it is the traditional family to which we still aspire. But is it really the case that children in other family forms are at risk of psychological harm? It seems not. Just because children are conceived in unusual ways, or live in unusual family circumstances, does not necessarily mean that they are more likely to grow up psychologically disturbed. Family structure, in itself, makes little difference to children's psychological development. Instead, what really matters is the quality of family life.

Families deviate from the norm in a variety of ways. As we have seen, a substantial minority of children are now raised by single mothers. Of these, some are reared by a lone mother from birth while others find themselves in this situation after their parents divorce. Stepfamilies are also becoming more common, with an increasing number of children moving in and out of different stepfamilies as they grow up. Although single-mother families are thought of as fatherless families, there is great diversity in the types of relationship which children in such families have with their fathers. For some, their father is no more than an anonymous sperm donor. They will never meet him or know anything about him. For others, their father is a prominent figure in their lives. He may not live with them but may have regular contact and be seen most definitely as a father in his children's eyes.

For children in two-parent families, the question of who is the child's father, or mother, is not always easy to answer. In families created by donor insemination it is the social father who brings the child up, and not the genetic father, who is known as dad. But in stepfather families it is often the genetic father who is thought of in this way even when the child has lived mainly with the stepfather and may have lost all contact with the genetic father. Similar situations arise for children conceived by egg donation, and for children raised by stepmothers. Children conceived using a donated egg think of their social mother as their mum whereas stepmothers tend to be even less accepted than stepfathers. And for children adopted early in life it is the adoptive parents, not the genetic parents, who are generally seen as mum and dad.

Why is it that the lack of a genetic link between one or both parents and the child in families resulting from assisted reproduction or early adoption does not prevent non-genetic parents being thought of as 'real' parents whereas children in stepfamilies are more likely to think of their genetic parent in this way than the step-parent who is bringing them up? Who the child considers to be a parent seems to depend more on the social than the genetic relationship between them. Whether or not there is a genetic bond, it is the mother and father with whom they experience their first parenting relationship who are usually most important to the child.

Surrogacy can result in even more complex family relationships. When children are born as a result of a surrogacy arrangement, the surrogate mother, who may also be the genetic mother of the child, often remains in contact with the family. There is also an increasing number of egg donation families where the egg donor, the child's genetic mother, is known to the child. Because it is not unusual for a surrogate mother or an egg donor to be a friend or relative of the child's parents, this situation is not uncommon. What this means for the children's sense of who is their 'real' mother, and the type of relationship the child develops with each mother, remains, as yet, to be seen.

Another way in which families differ from the norm is in the sexual orientation of the parents and, just like other non-traditional families, families headed by lesbian or gay parents come in a variety of forms. Some lesbian families have one parent while others have two. Some lesbian mothers enter into this type of family following a divorce bringing their children with them whereas other couples plan a family together once their relationship is established. And fathers may play an active role or none at all. Although families headed by gay men are extremely rare, a small but growing number of gay men have children with lesbian women and become highly involved fathers. Furthermore, many children remain in contact with their gay father after their parents' divorce.

What the various types of family discussed in this book have most in common is that they do not conform to the traditional family pattern. Otherwise, they are as different from each other as they are from the norm. The experiences of children raised by single mothers, lesbian mothers or by parents with whom they have no genetic link are not alike, and it cannot be assumed that the consequences for children of growing up in these different family types will be the same. Neither can it be assumed that the consequences for such children will necessarily be bad.

In Part I we saw, for example, that the negative effects of being raised in a single-parent family had more to do with the social disadvantage that accompanies single parenthood than the presence of only one parent in the family home. We also saw that fathers are not essential for children's development of a male or female identity.

Neither is it the case that a genetic link is necessary for a strong bond to form between children and their parents, and children raised by lesbian and gay parents do not differ from their counterparts from heterosexual homes. Whether children are raised by one parent or two, whether or not a father is present in the home, whether the child is genetically unrelated to one or both parents, and whether the parents are homosexual or heterosexual, makes little difference to children's emotional well-being. Family structure, in itself, is not a major determinant of children's psychological adjustment.

So how can the higher rates of problems among children in some types of non-traditional families be explained? The answer lies in the different experiences of children in different family types. The children most at risk are those in single-parent families and in stepfamilies – families in which children have commonly been exposed to hostility between their parents, their parents' separation or divorce, often resulting in a loss of social and financial support, and the transition to a stepfamily necessitating the negotiation of new family relationships. In contrast, children who lack a genetic link with the parents who have raised them from birth, or whose parents are lesbian or gay, are no more likely to experience psychological problems than children from traditional homes. It is what happens within families, not the way families are composed, that seems to matter most.

This does not mean that all children in single-parent families will experience problems, or that all children of lesbian mothers, or all children who are genetically unrelated to their parents, will function well. The outcomes for children of single mothers are best when the mother is financially secure and has a supportive network of family and friends, and when the children are given the opportunity to maintain a close relationship with the father who no longer lives with them following the parents' divorce. Among children of lesbian mothers, the outcomes are worst for those children whose mothers are insensitive to the difficulties they face as a result of prejudice from the outside world, and it is commonly believed that children who are not told that they are genetically unrelated to their parents may be at risk for emotional problems as they grow up. So the particular circumstances in which children in the same family type are raised, and the consequences of these circumstances for family life, will influence the outcome for the children concerned. Whether children within the same type of family will fare well or poorly depends not just on family structure but on how the particular family structure impacts upon the quality of family life.

Which aspects of family life promote children's healthy psychological development, and which have a damaging effect? In Part II we saw that the opportunity to form attachments to parents or other caretakers is fundamental to children's psychological well-being. But it is not just whether or not attachments are formed, but the type of attachments that children have to their parents that affects how they will function in childhood and adult life. Children who become securely attached feel better about themselves, and have better relationships with others, than those who develop insecure attachment relationships. And it is the quality of relationships between children and their parents, particularly how sensitive and responsive their parents are to them, that is the key factor in whether a child will become securely attached. Other aspects of parenting are important as well: the ability to administer discipline while remaining warm and affectionate has consistently been shown to result in better outcomes for the child.

We must also remember that relationships between children and their parents do not take place within a social vacuum. Parents who are in conflict, or who have psychological problems themselves, are less able to be effective mothers or fathers to their child. The social circumstances of the family, and the neighbourhood in which the family lives, also make a difference to the quality of family life. Poverty, and the social disadvantages that accompany it, is one of the most detrimental and pernicious influences faced by children today.

But children are not simply victims of circumstance. Their own behaviour towards others directly influences the behaviour of others towards them. In this way, children themselves play an active part in shaping their experiences. Not all children are crushed by adversity. Some can overcome even the most extreme difficulties to lead successful and fulfilling lives.

Although it used to be thought that what happened in the first few years of life determined a child's later development, the remarkable stories told by Ann and Alan Clarke of the recovery of children who moved to a warm and supportive family environment after suffering severe neglect or abuse, demonstrated that all is not lost even if the early years are bad.[1] Although these children were left with difficulties as they grew up, they benefited enormously from the improvement in their lives.

What about children who do not suffer extreme deprivation in their first years of life? Just how important is early experience for the later development of these more typical children? In order to address this question, researchers have carried out longitudinal studies, following up children from early childhood to adult life. What these studies tell us is that links do exist between childhood and adulthood, but is not the case that adverse early experiences inevitably cause irreversible damage. Instead, it seems that negative experiences in childhood trigger a chain of events that may result in psychological problems in adult life. However, if the child's circumstances improve, the course of his or her life may also change for the better.

This is demonstrated by David Quinton and Michael Rutter's study of children raised in institutions.[2] They found that some mothers whose children were being raised in institutions had themselves been reared under similar circumstances. When the chain of events leading to institutional care was examined in detail, it was found that the mothers had been placed in an institution as children because of their parents' inability to care for them. On leaving the institution in adolescence they either had no family to return to, or went back to the discordant family that they had previously left. Many soon became pregnant, or married early, to escape.

Often these marriages, entered into for negative reasons, broke down, or the women found themselves with unsupportive and hostile husbands and could not cope. As a consequence they were unable to function as parents and, with history repeating itself, their children entered institutional care.

Other studies have similarly pointed to links between experiences in childhood and outcomes in adult life that are not directly related but instead result from a sequence of events. Avshalom Caspi and his colleagues found that children who had temper tantrums in their early years had lower occupational status in middle age.[3] Temper tantrums did not lead directly to less successful careers. However, children who had temper tantrums were more likely to leave school early and consequently were less likely to show high educational attainment in early adulthood which mitigated against high status employment by middle age. Similarly, George Brown, Tirril Harris and Antonia Bifulco[4] have demonstrated that, for girls, a series of events beginning with separation from parents in childhood can lead to depression in adult life. Once again there was no direct link between the two. Instead, separation was associated with an increased risk of poor parenting which was related to a greater likelihood of premarital pregnancy, and girls in this situation were more likely to end up in a lower social class with an undependable husband. Poor parental care was also associated with feelings of helplessness for these girls. Lower social class, an undependable husband and feelings of helplessness were each associated with an increased likelihood of depression in adult life.

These studies are important not only because they show how negative events in childhood can lead to negative consequences in adult life but also because they demonstrate that improvements in the child's family circumstances can counteract the potential adverse effects of early negative experiences. In the study by David Quinton and Michael Rutter, the outcome was quite different for those girls who returned to a harmonious family in adolescence.[2] They were more likely to marry for positive reasons rather than to escape, and less likely to have a teenage pregnancy. As a result, they were more likely to become effective parents and less likely to have their children placed in institutional care. Similarly, in the investigation of the antecedents of depression among women, separation from parents in childhood carried no risk if did not lead to poor parental care.[4]

A major lesson to be learned from longitudinal research is that some children arrive in the same place by following the same route, some follow different routes to reach the same destination, some set out along the same route but branch off to arrive in different places, and others follow pathways that never meet. Although parents cannot determine the routes their children will take, they can influence them in one direction or another.

What really counts in being a good parent? Which parents facilitate the positive development of their children, and which parents inhibit them? In drawing conclusions about the influence of parents on children it is essential to be precise about just what aspects of parenting we are referring to – the type of family that parents provide or the quality of family relationships. It is no longer appropriate to assume that traditional families are good and non-traditional families bad for children. What matters most for children's psychological well-being is not family type – it is the quality of family life.

Notes

1 Number of parents: one versus two?

1 Rogers, B. and Pryor, J. (1998) *Divorce and Separation: The Outcomes for Children*. York: Joseph Rowntree Foundation.

2 Hetherington, E.M., Cox, M. and Cox, R. (1982) Effects of divorce on parents and children. In M.E. Lamb (ed.), *Nontraditional Families: Parenting and Child Development* (pp. 233–288). Hillsdale, NJ: Lawrence Erlbaum Associates.

3 Hetherington, E.M. (1988) Parents, children and siblings six years after divorce. In R.H.J. Stevenson-Hinde (ed.), *Relationships with Families* (pp. 311–331). Cambridge: Cambridge University Press.

4 Hetherington, E.M., Bridges, M. and Insabella, G.M. (1998) What matters? What does not? Five perspectives on the association between marital transitions and children's adjustment. *American Psychologist*, 53(2), 167–184.

5 Amato, P. (1993) Children's adjustment to divorce: theories, hypotheses, and empirical support. *Journal of Marriage and the Family*, 55, 23–38.

6 Cherlin, A., Furstenberg, F., Chase-Lansdale, P., Kiernan, K., Robins, P., Morrison, D. and Teitler, J. (1991) Longitudinal studies of effects of divorce on children in Great Britain and the United States. *Science*, 252, 1386–1389.

7 Ferri, E. (1976) *Growing up in a One Parent Family*. Slough: NFER.

8 McLanahan, S. and Sandefur, G. (1994) *Growing up with a Single Parent: What Hurts, what Helps*. Cambridge, MA: Harvard University Press.

9 Hetherington, E.M. and Stanley-Hagan, M.M. (1995) Parenting in divorced and remarried families. In M.H. Bornstein (ed.), *Handbook of Parenting* (Vol. 3, pp. 233–254). Hove, UK: Lawrence Erlbaum Associates.

10 Hetherington, E.M. and Stanley-Hagan, M. (1999) The adjustment of children with divorced parents: a risk and resiliency perspective. *Journal of Child Psychology and Psychiatry*, 40(1), 129–140.

11 Fidell, L. and Marik, J. (1989) Paternity by proxy: artificial insemination by donor sperm. In J. Offerman-Zuckerbery (ed.), *Gender in Transition: A New Frontier* (pp. 93–110). New York: Plenum.

12 Golombok, S., Tasker, F. and Murray, C. (1997). Children raised in fatherless

families from infancy: family relationships and the socioemotional development of children of lesbian and single heterosexual mothers. *Journal of Child Psychology and Psychiatry*, 38 (7), 783–792.

13 Weinraub, M. and Gringlas, M.B. (1995) Single parenthood. In M.H. Bornstein (ed.), *Handbook of Parenting* (Vol. 3, pp. 65–87). Hove, UK: Lawrence Erlbaum Associates.

2 Fathers: present or not?

1 Lamb, M.E. (1997) Fathers and child development: an introductory overview and guide. In M.E. Lamb (ed.), *The Role of the Father in Child Development* (pp. 1–18). New York: Wiley.

2 Lamb, M.E. (1986) Introduction: the emergent American father. In M.E. Lamb (ed.), *The Father's Role: Applied Perspectives*. New York: Wiley.

3 Pleck, J.H. (1997) Paternal involvement: levels, sources and consequences. In M.E. Lamb (ed.), *The Role of the Father in Child Development* (pp. 66–103). New York: Wiley.

4 Belsky, J. and Volling, B. (1987) Mothering, fathering, and marital interaction in the family triad during infancy: exploring family systems processes. In P.W. Berman and F.A. Pedersen (eds), *Men's Transitions to Parenthood: Longitudinal Studies of Early Family Experience* (pp. 37–63). Hillsdale, NJ: Lawrence Erlbaum Associates.

5 Lamb, M.E., Frodi, A., Hwang, C.P. and Frodi, M. (1982) Varying degrees of paternal involvement in infant care: attitudinal and behavioral correlates. In M.E. Lamb (ed.), *Nontraditional Families: Parenting and Child Development* (pp. 117–137). Hillsdale, NJ: Lawrence Erlbaum Associates.

6 Sagi, A. (1982) Antecedents and consequences of various degrees of paternal involvement in childrearing: the Israeli project. In M.E. Lamb (ed.), *Nontraditional Families: Parenting and Child Development* (pp. 205–232). Hillsdale, NJ: Lawrence Erlbaum Associates.

7 Russell, G. and Russell, A. (1987) Mother–child and father–child relationships in middle childhood. *Child Development*, 58, 1573–1585.

8 Hosley, C. and Montemayor, R. (1997) Father and adolescents. In M.E. Lamb (ed.), *The Role of the Father in Child Development* (pp. 162–178). New York: Wiley.

9 Lamb, M.E. (1997) The development of father–infant relationships. In M.E. Lamb (ed.), *The Role of the Father in Child Development* (pp. 104–120). New York: Wiley.

10 Parke, R.D. (1996) *Fatherhood*. Cambridge, MA: Harvard University Press.

11 Clarke-Stewart, K.A. (1980) The father's contribution to children's cognitive and social development in early childhood. In F.A. Pedersen (ed.), *The Father–Infant Relationship: Observational Studies in the Family Setting*. New York: Praeger.

12 Parke, R.D. and Sawin, D.B. (1980) The family in early infancy: social

interactional and attitudinal analyses. In F. Pedersen (ed.), *The Father–Infant Relationship: Observational Studies in a Family Context*. New York: Praeger.

13 Cox, M.J., Owen, M.T., Henderson, V.K. and Margand, N.A. (1992) Prediction of infant–mother and infant–father attachment. *Developmental Psychology*, 28, 474–483.

14 Stevenson, M.R. and Black, K.N. (1988) Parental absence and sex role development: a meta-analysis. *Child Development*, 59, 793–814.

15 Hetherington, E.M. and Stanley-Hagan, M.M. (1995) Parenting in divorced and remarried families. In M.H. Bornstein (ed.), *Handbook of Parenting* (Vol. 3, pp. 233–254). Hove, UK: Lawrence Erlbaum Associates.

16 Radin, N. (1994) Primary caregiving fathers in intact families. In A.E. Gottfried and A.W. Gottfried (eds), *Redefining Families* (pp. 237). New York: Plenum.

17 Suess, G., Grossman, K. and Sroufe, L.A. (1992) Effects of infant attachment to mother and father on quality of adaptation to preschool: from dynamic to individual organization of self. *International Journal of Behavioral Development*, 15, 43–65.

18 Youngblade, L.M. and Belsky, J. (1992). Parent–child antecedents of 5-year-olds' close friendships: a longitudinal analysis. *Developmental Psychology*, 28, 700–713.

19 Mosley, J. and Thomson, E. (1995) Fathering behavior and child outcomes: the role of race and poverty. In W. Marsiglio (ed.), *Fatherhood: Contemporary Theory, Research and Social Policy* (pp. 148–165). Thousand Oaks, CA: Sage.

20 Gottfried, A.E., Gottfried, A.W. and Bathurst, K. (1988) Maternal employment, family environment, and children's development. In A.E. Gottfried and A.W. Gottfried (eds), *Maternal Employment and Children's Development: Longitudinal Research* (pp. 11–58). New York: Plenum.

3 Genetic ties: related or not?

1 Levy-Shiff, R., Goldshmidt, I. and Har-Even, D. (1991) Transition to parenthood in adoptive families. *Developmental Psychology*, 27(1), 131–140.

2 Singer, L., Brodzinsky, D., Ramsay, D., Steir, M. and Waters, E. (1985) Mother–infant attachment in adoptive families. *Child Development*, 56, 1543–1551.

3 Brodzinsky, D.M., Lang, R. and Smith, D.W. (1995) Parenting adopted children. In M. Bornstein (ed.), *Handbook of Parenting* (Vol. 3, pp. 209–232). Hove, UK: Lawrence Erlbaum Associates.

4 Brodzinsky, D.M., Smith, D.W. and Brodzinsky, A.B. (1998) *Children's Adjustment to Adoption. Developmental and Clinical Issues* (Vol. 38). London: Sage Publications.

5 Grotevant, M.D. and McRoy, R.G. (1998) *Openness in Adoption: Exploring Family Connections*. New York: Sage.

6 Daniels, K. and Taylor, K. (1993) Secrecy and openness in donor insemination. *Politics and Life Sciences*, 12 (2), 155–170.
7 Cook, R. and Golombok, S. (1995) A survey of semen donors: phase II – the view of the donors. *Human Reproduction*, 10, 951–959.
8 Clamar, A. (1988) Psychological implications of the anonymous pregnancy. In J. Offerman-Zuckerberg (ed.), *Gender in Transition: A New Frontier*. New York: Plenum.
9 Golombok, S., Brewaeys, A., Cook, R., Giavazzi, M.T., Guerra, D., Mantovanni, A., Van Hall, E., Crosignano, P.G. and Dexeus, S. (1996) The European Study of Assisted Reproduction Families. *Human Reproduction*, 11 (10), 2324–2331.
10 Trouson, A., Leeton, J., Besanka, M., Wood, C. and Conti, A. (1983) Pregnancy established in an infertile patient after transfer of a donated embryo fertilized in vitro. *British Medical Journal*, 286, 835–838.
11 Golombok, S., Murray, C., Brinsden, P., and Abdalla, H. (1999) Social versus biological parenting: family functioning and the socioemotional development of children conceived by egg or sperm donation. *Journal of Child Psychology and Psychiatry*, 40 (4), 519–527.
12 Brazier, M., Campbell, A. and Golombok, S. (1998) *Surrogacy: Review for Health Ministers of Current Arrangements for Payments and Regulation* (Cmd. 4068). London: Department of Health.
13 Hetherington, E.M. (1989) Coping with family transitions: winners, losers, and survivors. *Child Development*, 60, 1–14.
14 Hetherington, E.M. (1988) Parents, children and siblings six years after divorce. In R. Hinde and J. Stevenson-Hinde (eds), *Relationships with Families*. Cambridge: Cambridge University Press.
15 Hetherington, E.M. and Clingempeel, W.G. (1992) *Coping with Marital Transitions*. Monographs of the Society for Research in Child Development (Vol. 57, Nos. 2–3).
16 Hetherington, E.M. and Stanley-Hagan, M.M. (1995). Parenting in divorced and remarried families. In M.H. Bornstein (ed.), *Handbook of Parenting* (Vol. 3, pp. 233–254.). Hove, UK: Lawrence Erlbaum Associates.
17 Dunn, J., Deater-Deckard, K., Pickering, K., O'Connor, T.G., Golding, J. and the ALSPAC Study Team (1998) Children's adjustment and prosocial behaviour in step- , single-parent, and non-stepfamily settings: findings from a community study. *Journal of Child Psychology and Psychiatry*, 39 (8), 1083–1095.

4 Parents' sexual orientation: heterosexual or homosexual?

1 Patterson, C.J. (1992) Children of lesbian and gay parents. *Child Development*, 63, 1025–1042.
2 Golombok, S. (1999) Lesbian mother families. In A. Bainham, S. Day Sclater and M. Richards (eds), *What is a Parent? A Socio-legal Analysis* (pp. 161–180) Oxford: Hart.

3 Golombok, S. and Fivush, R. (1994) *Gender Development*. New York: Cambridge University Press.

4 Collaer, M.L. and Hines, M. (1995) Human behavioral sex differences: a role for gonadal hormones during early development? *Psychological Bulletin*, 118 (1), 55–107.

5 Money, J. and Ehrhardt, A. (1972) *Man and Woman, Boy and Girl: The Differentiation and Dimorphism of Gender Identity from Conception to Maturity.* Baltimore, MD: Johns Hopkins University Press.

6 Diamond, M. and Sigmundson, H.K. (1997) Sex reassignment at birth: long-term review and clinical implications. *Archives of Pediatric Medicine*, 151, 298–304.

7 Imperato-McGinley, J., Peterson, R.E., Gautier, T. and Sturla, E. (1979) Androgens and the evolution of male gender identity among male pseudohermaphrodites with 5α reductase deficiency. *New England Journal of Medicine*, 300, 1233–1237.

8 Bailey, J.M. and Pillard, R.C. (1991) A genetic study of male sexual orientation. *Archives of General Psychiatry*, 48, 1089–1096.

9 Bailey, J.M., Pillard, R.C., Neale, M.C. and Ageyei, Y. (1993) Heritable factors influence sexual orientation in women. *Archives of General Psychiatry*, 50, 217–223.

10 Hamer, D., Hu, S., Magnuson, V., Hu, N. and Pattatucci, A. (1993) A linkage between DNA markers on the X chromosome and male sexual orientation. *Science*, 261, 321–327.

11 Ehrhardt, A., Meyer-Bahlburg, H., Rosen, L., Feldman, J., Veridiano, N., Zimmerman, I. and McEwen, B. (1985) Sexual orientation after prenatal exposure to exogenous estrogen. *Archives of Sexual Behavior*, 14, 57–77.

12 Green, R. (1987) *The 'Sissy Boy Syndrome' and the Development of Homosexuality*. New Haven, CT: Yale University Press.

13 Freud, S. (1905/1953) *Three Essays on the Theory of Sexuality* (Vol. 7). London: Hogarth Press.

14 Freud, S. (1933) *Psychology of Women: New Introductory Lectures on Psychoanalysis*. London: Hogarth Press.

15 Bandura, A. (1977) *Social Learning Theory*. Englewood Cliffs, NJ: Prentice Hall.

16 Mischel, W. (1970) Sex-typing and socialization. In P. Mussen (ed.), *Carmichael's Manual of Child Psychology* (Vol. 2, pp. 3–72). New York: Wiley.

17 Fagot, B.I. (1978) The influence of sex of child on parental reactions to toddler children. *Child Development*, 49, 459–465.

18 Bandura, A. (1986) *Social Foundations of Thought and Action: A Social Cognitive Theory*. Englewood Cliffs, NJ: Prentice Hall.

19 Martin, C.L. (1993) New directions for assessing children's gender knowledge. *Developmental Review*, 13 (2), 184–204.

20 Golombok, S., Spencer, A. and Rutter, M. (1983) Children in lesbian and

single-parent households: psychosexual and psychiatric appraisal. *Journal of Child Psychology and Psychiatry*, 24, 551–572.

21 Green, R., Mandel, J.B., Hotvedt, M.E., Gray, J. and Smith, L. (1986) Lesbian mothers and their children: a comparison with solo parent heterosexual mothers and their children. *Archives of Sexual Behavior*, 15, 167–184.

22 Kirkpatrick, M., Smith, C. and Roy, R. (1981) Lesbian mothers and their children: a comparative survey. *American Journal of Orthopsychiatry*, 51, 545–551.

23 Tasker, F. and Golombok, S. (1997) *Growing up in a Lesbian Family*. New York: Guilford Press.

24 Brewaeys, A., Ponjaert, I., van Hall, E. and Golombok, S. (1997) Donor insemination: child development and family functioning in lesbian mother families. *Human Reproduction*, 12 (6), 1349–1359.

25 Flaks, D.K., Ficher, I., Masterpasqua, F. and Joseph, G. (1995) Lesbians choosing motherhood: a comparative study of lesbian and heterosexual parents and their children. *Developmental Psychology*, 31, 105–114.

26 Chan, R.W., Raboy, B. and Patterson, C.J. (1998) Psychosocial adjustment among children conceived via donor insemination by lesbian and heterosexual mothers. *Child Development*, 69 (2), 443–457.

27 Golombok, S., Tasker, F. and Murray, C. (1997) Children raised in fatherless families from infancy: family relationships and the socioemotional development of children of lesbian and single heterosexual mothers. *Journal of Child Psychology and Psychiatry*, 38 (7), 783–792.

28 Brewaeys, A., Ponjaert-Kristoffersen, I,. van Steirteghem, A.C. and de Vroey, P. (1993) Children from anonymous donors: an inquiry into heterosexual and homosexual parents' attitudes. *Journal of Psychosomatic Obstetrics and Gynaecology*, 14, 23–35.

29 Golombok, S. and Tasker, F. (1994) Children in lesbian and gay families: theories and evidence. *Annual Review of Sex Research*, 5, 73–100.

5 Quality of relationships between parents and children

1 Bowlby, J. (1969) *Attachment and Loss. Volume 1. Attachment*. London: Hogarth Press.

2 Bowlby, J. (1951) *Maternal Care and Mental Health*. Geneva: World Health Organization.

3 Bowlby, J. (1988) *A Secure Base: Clinical Applications of Attachment Theory*. London: Routledge.

4 Bowlby, J. (1944) Forty-four juvenile thieves: their characters and home life. *International Journal of Psycho-Analysis*, 25, 19–52.

5 Harlow, H. and Harlow, M. (1969) Effects of various mother–infant relationships on rhesus monkey behaviours. In B. M. Foss (ed.), *Determinants of Infant Behaviour* (Vol. 4). London: Methuen.

6 Goldfarb, W. (1947) Variations of adolescent adjustment of institutionally reared children. *Americal Journal of Orthopsychiatry*, 17, 449–457.

7 Chisholm, K. (1998) A three year follow-up of attachment and indiscriminate friendliness in children adopted from Romanian orphanages. *Child Development*, 69 (4), 1092–1106.

8 Ainsworth, M.D.S. and Wittig, B.A. (1969) Attachment and exploratory behavior of one-year-olds in a strange situation. In B.M. Foss (ed.), *Determinants of Infant Behaviour* (Vol. 4, pp. 113–136). London: Methuen.

9 Main, M. and Solomon, J. (1990) Procedures for identifying infants as disorganised/ disoriented during the Ainsworth Strange Situation. In M.T. Greenberg, D. Cicchetti and E.M. Cummings (eds), *Attachment in the Preschool Years* (pp. 121–160). Chicago, IL: University of Chicago Press.

10 Belsky, J. and Rovine, M. (1987) Temperament and attachment security in the Strange Situation: an empirical rapprochement. *Child Development*, 58, 787–795.

11 van IJzendoorn, M.H. and De Wolff, M.S. (1997) In search of the absent father – meta-analyses of infant–father attachment: A rejoinder to our discussants. *Child Development*, 68 (4), 604–609.

12 Erickson, M.A., Sroufe, L.A. and Egeland, B. (1985) The relationship between quality of attachment and behaviour in preschool in a high risk sample. In I. Bretherton and E. Waters (eds), *Growing Points in Attachment Theory and Research*. Monographs of the Society for Research in Child Development, 50 (1–2, Serial no. 209), pp. 147–166.

13 Sroufe, L.A. (1986) Appraisal: Bowlby's contribution to psychoanalytic theory and developmental psychology: attachment: separation: loss. *Journal of Child Psychology and Psychiatry*, 27, 841–849.

14 Suess, G., Grossman, K. and Sroufe, L.A. (1992) Effects of infant attachment to mother and father on quality of adaptation to preschool: from dynamic to individual organization of self. *International Journal of Behavioral Development*, 15, 43–65.

15 Youngblade, L.M. and Belsky, J. (1992) Parent–child antecedents of 5-year-olds' close friendships: A longitudinal analysis. *Developmental Psychology*, 28, 700–713.

16 Belsky, J. and Cassidy, J. (1994) Attachment: theory and evidence. In M. Rutter and D. Hay (eds), *Development Through Life: A Handbook for Clinicians* (pp. 373–402). Oxford: Blackwell Scientific Publications.

17 Lewis, M., Feiring, C., McGuffog, C. and Jaskir, J. (1984) Predicting psychopathology in six-year-olds from early social relations. *Child Development*, 123–136.

18 Crockenberg, S. (1981) Infant irritability, mother responsiveness, and social support influences on the security of infant–mother attachment. *Child Development*, 52, 857–865.

19 Ainsworth, M., Blehar, M., Waters, E. and Wall, S. (1978) *Patterns of*

Attachment: A Psychological Study of the Strange Situation. Hillsdale, NJ.: Lawrence Erlbaum Associates.

20 Ainsworth, M. (1985) Patterns of infant–mother attachments: antecedents and effects on development. *Bulletin of New York Academy of Medicine*, 66 (9), 771–790.

21 Steele, H. and Steele, M. (1994) Intergenerational patterns of attachment. In D. Perlman and K. Bartholomew (eds), *Attachment Processes during Adulthood* (pp. 93–120). London: Jessica Kingsley.

22 De Wolff, M.S. and van IJzendoorn, M.H. (1997) Sensitivity and attachment: a meta-analysis on parental antecedents of infant attachment. *Child Development*, 68 (4), 571–591.

23 Main, M., Kaplan, N. and Cassidy, J. (1985) Security in infancy, childhood, and adulthood: a move to the level of representation. In I. Bretherton and E. Waters (eds), *Growing Points in Attachment Theory and Research*. Monographs of the Society for Research in Child Development, 50 (1–2, Serial no. 209), pp. 66–104.

24 Main, M. and Cassidy, J. (1988) Categories of response to reunion with the parent at age 6: predictable from infant attachment classifications and stable over a 1-month period. *Developmental Psychology*, 24 (3), 415–426.

25 Grossmann, K.E. and Grossmann, K. (1991) Attachment quality as an organizer of emotional and behavioural responses in a longitudinal perspective. In C.M. Parkes, J. Stevenson-Hinde and P. Marris (eds), *Attachment across the Life Cycle* (pp. 93–114). London: Routledge.

26 George, C., Kaplan, N. and Main, M. (1985) Adult Attachment Interview. Unpublished Manuscript, University of California, Berkeley.

27 van Izendoorn, M.H. (1995) Adult attachment representations, parental responsiveness, and infant attachment: a meta-analysis on the predictive validity of the Adult Attachment Interview. *Psychological Bulletin*, 117 (3), 387–403.

28 Fonagy, P., Steele, H. and Steele, M. (1991). Maternal representations of attachment during pregnancy predict the organization of infant–mother attachment at one year of age. *Child Development*, 62, 891–905.

29 Fox, N. (1995) Of the way we were: adult memories about attachment experiences and their role in determining infant–parent relationships: a commentary on van IJzendoorn (1995). *Psychological Bulletin*, 117(3), 304–410.

30 Cassidy, J. and Shaver, P.R. (1999) *Handbook of Attachment: Theory, Research and Clinical Applications*. New York: Guilford Press.

6 Quality of marriage and parents' psychological state

1 Gottman, J.M. (1979) *Marital Interaction: Experimental Investigations*. San Diego, CA: Academic Press.

2 Gottman, J.M. (1994) *What Predicts Divorce?* Hillsdale, NJ: Lawrence Erlbaum Associates.

3 Fincham, F.D. and Osborne, L.N. (1993) Marital conflict and children: retrospect and prospect. *Clinical Psychology Review*, 13, 75–88.

4 Grych, J.H. and Fincham, F.D. (1990) Marital conflict and children's adjustment: a cognitive-contextual framework. *Psychological Bulletin*, 108 (2), 267–290.

5 Cummings, E.M. and Davies, P. (1994). *Children and Marital Conflict*. New York: Guilford Press.

6 Emery, R.E. (1988) *Marriage, Divorce and Children's Adjustment*. Newbury Park, CA: Sage.

7 Moffitt, T.E. and Caspi, A. (1998). Annotation: implications of violence between intimate partners for child psychologists and psychiatrists. *Journal of Child Psychology and Psychiatry*, 39 (2), 137–144.

8 Grych, J.H. and Fincham, D.F. (1993) Children's appraisals of marital conflict: initial investigations of the cognitive-contextual framework. *Child Development*, 64, 215–230.

9 Davies, P.T. and Cummings, E.M. (1994). Marital conflict and child adjustment: an emotional security hypothesis. *Psychological Bulletin*, 116 (3), 387–411.

10 Fauber, R.L. and Long, N. (1991) Children in context: the role of the family in child psychotherapy. *Journal of Consulting and Clinical Psychology*, 59, 813–820.

11 Baumrind, D. (1989) Rearing competent children. In W. Damon (ed.), *Child Development Today and Tomorrow* (pp. 349–378). San Fransisco, CA: Jossey-Bass.

12 Patterson, G.R. (1982) *Coercive Family Process*. Eugene, OR: Castalia.

13 Patterson G.R., Reid., J.B. and Dishion, T.J. (1992) *Antisocial Boys*. Eugene, OR: Castalia.

14 Stoneman, Z., Brody, G.H. and Burke, M. (1989) Marital quality, depression and inconsistent parenting: relationship with observed mother–child conflict. *American Journal of Orthopsychiatry*, 59 (1), 105–117.

15 Howes, P. and Markman, H.J. (1989) Marital quality and child functioning: a longitudinal investigation. *Child Development*, 60, 1044–1051.

16 Coiro, M.J. and Emery, R.E. (1998) Do marriage problems affect fathering more than mothering? A quantitative and qualitative review. *Clinical Child and Family Psychology Review*, 1 (1), 23–39.

17 Harold, G.T. and Conger, R.D. (1997) Marital conflict and adolescent distress: the role of adolescent awareness. *Child Development*, 68 (2), 333–350.

18 Weissman, M.M., Prusoff, B.A., Gammon, G.D., Merikangas, K.R., Leckman, J.F. and Kidd, K.K. (1984) Psychopathology in the children (ages 6–18) of depressed and normal parents. *Journal of the American Academy of Child Psychiatry*, 23, 78–84.

19 Weissman, M.M., Gammon, G.D., John, K., Kerikangas, K.R., Prusoff, B.A. and Sholomskas, D. (1987) Children of depressed parents: increased psychopathology and early onset of major depression. *Archives of General Psychiatry*, 44, 847–853.

20 Weissman, M.M., Warner, V., Wickramaratne, P., Moreau, D. and Olfson, M. (1997) Offspring of depressed parents: ten years later. *Archives of General Psychiatry*, 54(10), 932–940.

21 Hammen, C., Gordon, G., Burge, D., Adrian, C., Jaenicke, C. and Hirito, G. (1987) Maternal affective disorders, illness, and stress: risk for children's psychopathology. *American Journal of Psychiatry*, 144, 736–741.

22 Orvaschel, H., Walsh-Altis, G. and Ye, W. (1988) Psychopathology in children of parents with recurrent depression. *Journal of Abnormal Child Psychology*, 16, 17–28.

23 Cummings, E.M. and Davies, P.T. (1994) Maternal depression and child development. *Journal of Child Psychology and Psychiatry*, 35 (1), 73–112.

24 Kochanska, G., Kuczynski, L., Radke-Yarrow, M. and Welsh, J.D. (1987) Resolution of control episodes between well and affectively ill mothers and their young child. *Journal of Abnormal Child Psychology*, 15, 441–456.

25 Tronick, E.Z. (1989) Emotions and emotional communication in infants. *American Psychologist*, 44, 112–119.

26 Jameson, P.B., Gelfand, D., Kulcsar, E. and Teti, D. (1997) Mother–toddler interaction patterns associated with maternal depression. *Development and Psychopathology*, 9, 537–550.

27 Field, T. (1995) Psychologically depressed parents. In M. Bornstein (ed.), *Handbook of Parenting* (Vol. 4, 85–99). Hove, UK: Lawrence Erlbaum Associates.

28 Murray, L. (1992) The impact of post-natal depression on mother–infant relations and infant development. *Journal of Child Psychology and Psychiatry*, 33, 543–561.

29 Radke-Yarrow, M., Cummings, E.M., Kuczynski, L. and Chapman, M. (1985) Patterns of attachment in two- and three-year-olds in normal families and families with parental depression. *Child Development*, 56, 884–893.

30 Emery, R., Weintraub, S. and Neale, J.M. (1982) Effects of marital discord on the school behaviour of children of schizophrenic, affectively disordered and normal parents. *Journal of Abnormal Child Psychology*, 10, 215–228.

31 Cox, A.D., Puckering, C., Pound, A. and Mills, M. (1987). The impact of maternal depression in young people. *Journal of Child Psychology and Psychiatry*, 28, 917–928.

32 Downey, G. and Coyne, J.C. (1990). Children of depressed parents: an integrative review. *Psychological Bulletin*, 108, 50–76.

33 McGuffin, P., Katz, R., Watkins, S. and Rutherford, J. (1996) A hospital-based twin registery study of the heritability of DSM-IV unipolar depression. *Archives of General Psychiatry*, 53, 129–136.

34 Weintraub, S. (1987) Risk factors in schizophrenia: the Stony Brook High-Risk Project. *Schizophrenia Bulletin*, 13, 439–449.

35 Goodman, S. (1987) Emory University project on children of disturbed parents. *Schizophrenia Bulletin*, 13, 412–423.

36 Erlenmeyer-Kimling, L. and Cornblatt, B. (1987) The New York High-Risk Project. *Schizophrenia Bulletin*, 13, 451–461.

37 Tienari, P., Sorri, A., Lahti, I., Naarala, M., Wahlberg, K.E., Morig, J., Pohjola, J. and Wynne, L.C. (1987) Genetic and psychosocial factors in schizophrenia: the Finnish Adoptive Family Study. *Schizophrenia Bulletin*, 13, 477–484.

38 Mayes, L.C. (1995) Substance abuse and parenting. In M. Bornstein (ed.), *Handbook of Parenting* (Vol. 4, pp. 101–125). Hove, UK: Lawrence Erlbaum Associates.

39 Wilson, G.S. (1989) Clinical studies of infants and children exposed prenatally to heroin. *Annals of the New York Academy of Science*, 562, 183–194.

40 Schuckit, M. and Smith, T. (1996) An 8-year follow-up of 450 sons of alcoholic and control subjects. *Archives of General Psychiatry*, 53, 202–210.

41 Singer, L., Arendt, R., Farkas, K., Minnes, S., Huang, J. and Yamashita, T. (1997) Relationship of prenatal cocaine exposure and maternal postpartum psychological distress to child developmental outcome. *Development and Psychopathology*, 9, 473–489.

42 Dunn, J. and McGuire, S. (1992) Sibling and peer relationships in childhood. *Journal of Child Psychology and Psychiatry*, 33, 67–105.

43 Dunn, J., Deater-Deckard, K., Pickering, K., Golding, J. and the ALSPAC Study Team (1999) Siblings, parents, and partners: family relationships within a longitudinal community study. *Journal of Child Psychology and Psychiatry*, 40, 1025–1037.

44 Jenkins, J.M. (1992) Sibling relationships in disharmonious homes: potential difficulties and protective effects. In F. Boer and J. Dunn (eds), *Children's Sibling Relationships: Developmental and Clinical Issues* (pp. 125–138). Hillsdale, NJ: Lawrence Erlbaum Associates.

7 Children's individual characteristics and their wider social world

1 Scarr, S. (1998) American child care today. *American Psychologist*, 52 (2), 95–108.

2 Scarr, S. and Eisenberg, M. (1993) Child care research: issues, perspectives, and results. *Annual Review of Psychology*, 44, 613–644.

3 Goossens, F.A. and van IJzendoorn, M.H. (1990) Quality of infants' attachments to professional caregivers: relation to infant–parent attachment and day-care characteristics. *Child Development*, 61, 550–567.

4 Howes, C. and Hamilton, C.E. (1992) Children's relationships with child care teachers: stability and concordance with parental attachments. *Child Development*, 63, 867–878.

5 Belsky, J. (1988) Infant day care and socioemotional development in the United States. *Journal of Child Psychology and Psychiatry*, 29 (4), 397–406.

6 Fox, N.A. and Fein, G.G. (1989) *Infant Day Care: The Current Debate.* Norwood, NJ: Ablex Publishing Corporation.

7 NICHD Early Child Care Research Network (1997) The effects of infant child care on mother–infant attachment security: results of the NICHD study of early child care. *Child Development*, 68 (5), 860–879.

8 McCartney, K. (1984) The effect of quality of day care environment upon children's language development. *Developmental Psychology*, 20, 244–260.

9 Phillips, D.A., McCartney, K. and Scarr, S. (1987) Child care quality and children's social development. *Developmental Psychology*, 23, 537–543.

10 NICHD Early Child Care Research Network (1997) Mother–child interaction and cognitive outcomes associated with early child care: Results of the NICHD study. Paper presented at the Biennial meeting of the Society for Research in Child Development, Washington DC.

11 Zigler, E. and Styfco, S.J. (1994) Head start: criticisms in a constructive context. *American Psychologist*, 49 (2), 127–132.

12 Gottfried, A.E., Gottfried, A.W. and Bathurst, K. (1988) Maternal employment, family environment, and children's development: infancy through the school years. In A.E. Gottfried and A.W. Gottfried (eds), *Maternal Employment and Children's Development: Longitudinal Research* (11–58). New York: Plenum Press.

13 Howes, C. (1988) Relations between early child care and schooling. *Developmental Psychology*, 24, 53–57.

14 Terry, R. and Coie, J.D. (1991) A comparison of methods for defining sociometric status among children. *Developmental Psychology*, 27, 867–880.

15 Newcomb, A.F., Bukowski, W.M. and Pattee, L. (1993) Children's peer relations: a meta-analytic review of popular, rejected, neglected, controversial, and average sociometric status. *Psychological Bulletin*, 113 (1), 99–128.

16 Coie, J. D., Dodge, K.A. and Kupersmidt, J.B. (1990) Peer group behavior and social status. In S. R. Asher and J. D. Coie (eds), *Peer Rejection in Childhood* (pp. 17–59). New York: Cambridge University Press.

17 Dodge, K.A. and Feldman, E. (1990) Issues in social cognition and sociometric status. In S. R. Asher and J. D. Coie (eds), *Peer Rejection in Childhood* (p. 119–155). New York: Cambridge University Press.

18 Parkhurst, J.T. and Asher, S.R. (1992) Peer rejection in middle school: subgroup differences in behavior, loneliness, and interpersonal concerns. *Developmental Psychology*, 28, 231–241.

19 Ladd, G.W. (1990) Having friends, keeping friends, making friends, and being liked by peers in the classroom: predictors of children's early school adjustment. *Child Development*, 61, 1081–1100.

20 DeRosier, M.E., Kupersmidt, J.B. and Patterson, C.J. (1994) Children's academic and behavioral adjustment as a function of the chronicity and proximity of peer rejection. *Child Development*, 65, 1799–1813.

21 Coie, J.D., Coie, J.E., Lochman, R., Terry, R. and Hyman C. (1992) Predicting early adolescent disorder from childhood aggression and peer rejection. *Journal of Consulting and Clinical Psychology*, 60, 783–792.

22 Parker, J.G. and Asher, S.R. (1987) Peer relations and later personal adjustment: are low accepted children at risk? *Psychological Bulletin*, 102, 357–389.

23 Parker, J. and Asher, S. (1993) Friendship and friendship quality in middle childhood: links with peer group acceptance and feelings of loneliness and social dissatisfaction. *Developmental Psychology*, 29, 611–621.

24 Hartup, W.W. (1996) The company they keep: friendships and their developmental significance. *Child Development*, 67 (1), 1–13.

25 Parke, R. and Ladd, G. (ed.) (1992) *Family–Peer Relationships: Modes of Linkage*. Hillsdale, NJ: Lawrence Erlbaum Associates.

26 Patterson G.R., Reid, J.B. and Dishion, T.J. (1992) *Antisocial Boys*. Eugene, OR: Castalia.

27 Dishion, T.J., Patterson, G.R., Stoolmiller, M. and Skinner, M.L. (1991) Family, school, and behavioral antecedents to early adolescent involvement with antisocial peers. *Developmental Psychology*, 27 (1), 172–180.

28 McLoyd, V. (1998) Socioeconomic disadvantage and child development. *American Psychologist*, 53 (2), 185–204.

29 Conger, R., Conger, K., Elder, G., Lorenz, F., Simons, R. and Whitbeck, L. (1992) A family process model of economic hardship and adjustment of early adolescent boys. *Child Development*, 63, 526–541.

30 Conger, R., Ge, X., Elder, G., Lorenz, F. and Simons, R. (1994) Economic stress, coercive family process, and developmental problems of adolescents. *Child Development*, 65, 541–561.

31 Sampson, R. and Laub, J. (1994) Urban poverty and the family context of delinquency: a new look at structure and process in a classic study. *Child Development*, 65(2), 523–540.

32 Zimmerman, M.A. and Arunkumar, R. (1994) Resiliency research: implications for schools and policy. *Social Policy Report: Society for Research in Child Development*, Vol. 8, pp. 1–17.

33 Masten, A. and Coatsworth, J. (1998) The development of competence in favorable and unfavorable environments. *American Psychologist*, 53 (2), 205–220.

34 Werner, E.E. and Smith, R.S. (1992) *Overcoming the Odds: High Risk Children from Birth to Adulthood*. Ithaca, NY: Cornell University Press.

35 Thomas, A., Chess, S., Birch, H., Hertzig, M. and Korn, S. (1963) *Behavioral Individuality in Early Childhood*. New York: New York University Press.

36 Goldsmith, H., Buss, A., Plomin, R., Rothbart, M., Thomas, A., Chess, S., Hinde, R. and McCall, R. (1987) Roundtable: what is temperament? Four approaches. *Child Development*, 58, 505–529.

37 Kohnstamm, G.A., Bates, J.E. and Rothbart, M.K. (eds) (1989) *Temperament in Childhood*. Chichester, Sussex: John Wiley & Sons.

38 Plomin, R. (1990) *Nature and Nurture: An Introduction to Human Behavioral Genetics*. Pacific Grove, CA: Brooks/Cole.

39 Plomin, R. (1994) The Emanual Miller Memorial Lecture 1993. Genetic research and identification of environmental influences. *Journal of Child Psychology and Psychiatry*, 35 (5), 817–834.

40 Rutter, M., Silberg, J., O'Connor, T. and Simonoff, E. (1999) Genetics and child psychiatry: I Advances in quantative and molecular genetics. *Journal of Child Psychology and Psychiatry*, 40(1), 3–18.

41 Rutter, M., Silberg, J., O'Connor, T. and Simonoff, E. (1999) Genetics and child psychiatry: II Empirical research findings. *Journal of Child Psychology and Psychiatry*, 40(1), 19–55.

42 Collins, W.A., Maccoby, E., Steinberg, L., Hetherington, E.M. and Bornstein, M.H. (2000) Contemporary research on parenting: The case for nature and nurture. *American Psychology*, 55, 218–232.

43 DeFries, J., Plomin, R. and Fulker, D. (1993) *Nature and Nurture during Infancy and early Childhood*.

44 Plomin, R. and Daniels, D. (1987) Why are children in the same family so different from one another? *Behavioural and Brain Sciences*, 10, 1–16.

45 Dunn, J. and Plomin, R. (1990) *Separate Lives: Why Siblings are so Different*. New York: Basic Books.

8 Parenting: what really counts?

1 Clarke, A.D.B. and Clarke, A.M. (1976) *Early Experience: Myth and Evidence*. London: Open Books.

2 Quinton, D. and Rutter, M. (1988) *Parenting Breakdown: The Making and Breaking of Intergenerational Links*. Aldershot, Hants: Avebury Gower Publishing.

3 Caspi, A., Elder, G. and Herbener, E. (1990) Childhood personality and the prediction of life course patterns. In L. Robins and M. Rutter (eds), *Straight and Devious Pathways from Childhood to Adulthood* (pp. 13–35). Cambridge: Cambridge University Press.

4 Brown, G.W., Harris, T. and Bifulco, A. (1986) The long term effects of early loss of a parent. In M. Rutter, C.E. Izard and P. Read (eds), *Depression in Young People*. New York: Guilford Press.

Names index

Subject index